REAL REVIVAL: FROM ROOTS TO FRUITS

MARK ENDRES

COPYRIGHT

This product is available at quantity discounts.
info@handofjesus.org

REAL REVIVAL: FROM ROOTS TO FRUITS by Mark Endres

ISBN: 978-0-9893815-5-0 2nd Edition 2021

Scripture quotations marked NIV are from the New International Version. Copyright © 1973, 1978, 1984, International Bible Society. Used by permission.

Scripture quotations marked ISV are from the International Standard Version. Copyright © 1995-2014 by ISV Foundation.

Scripture quotations marked NIVUK are from the New International Version® Anglicized, NIV® Copyright © 1979, 1984, 2011 by Biblica, Inc.® Used by permission.

Scripture quotations marked AMP are from the Amplified Bible. Old Testament copyright © 1965, 1987 by Zondervan Corporation. The Amplified New Testament copyright © 1954, 1958, 1987 by the Lockman Foundation. Used by permission.

Scripture quotations marked NAS are from the New American Standard Bible, copyright © 1960, 1962, 1963, 1968, 1971, 1972, 1973, 1975, 1977, 1995 by The Lockman Foundation.

Scripture quotations marked NKJV are from the New King James Version of the Bible. Copyright © 1979, 1980, 1982 by Thomas Nelson, Inc., publishers. Used by permission.

Scripture quotations marked ESV are from The English Standard Version with the permission of Good News Publishers.

Cover design by: Angela R. Garrett

Tree Photo © Leonello Calvetti | Dreamstime.com

Visit the author's website at www.handofjesus.org

CONTENTS

DEDICATIONS

I dedicate this book to Tammy J. Endres.

I wrote the following and presented it to Tammy
on Sunday morning April 5th, 1987:

Strength and Weakness
Success and Failure
Courage and Fear
Joy and Sorrow
Wisdom and Ignorance
Patience and Anxiousness
Service and Rebellion
Commitment and Doubt
Good and Evil
Life and Death

All of our pilgrimage with Jesus shall bear forth the above. He will ever bid us to follow His path. As well-known is this path to Him, we stumble blindly depending completely on His guidance.
Daughter of God I come before you this day to ask:
Will you share my pilgrimage with Jesus?
I come asking: Can I share in yours?
I come by faith knowing that today is the appointed day to ask:
"Will you marry me?"
This is not a question based merely on emotion. It is not a question founded on human need. It is a question rooted firmly in divine declaration!
I believe we have been called to be helpmates to one another and therefore may God give you assurance this day.
I love you Tammy
Mark

I dedicate this book to You Heavenly Father.

I worship You. I thank You for speaking and giving me the courage and faith to please You. I am indebted to You for my very life. It is a joy to trust You.

PREFACE

If we would just have REAL REVIVAL!

Perhaps you have heard this statement. Perhaps you have made this statement. Perhaps you have led devotionals or preached messages related to this statement. I would suggest that anyone who has:

1) Received Jesus Christ as Savior and Lord, **and**

2) Pursued a sacrificial lifestyle of serving others

will indeed experience (or has already experienced) this desperate heart-felt cry for more of God's direct intervention into the affairs of men, women, children, families, cities, and nations.

When attempting to serve and meet the needs of others, we may find ourselves fighting challenging thoughts. Statements and questions produced by these thoughts may include:

- "If God would only…," **or**
- "Why does God continue to allow…," **or**
- "Doesn't God see…," **or**
- "Can't God…," **or**
- "If I were God, I would…," **or**
- "Didn't God say…." **or**

These statements are revealing. They drive us to a place of holy discontentment and create a God given cry in us. They produce a groaning, a longing, and a sighing.

Like the words of King David:

> *Now I am feeble and utterly crushed; I* ***groan*** *in anguish of heart. All my* ***longings*** *lie open before you, Lord; my* ***sighing*** *is not hidden from you.* —Psalm 38:8-9, emphasis added

Our desperation in prayer reflects the truth of Proverbs 13:12:

> *Hope deferred makes the heart sick, but a longing fulfilled is a tree of life.*

God, our heavenly Father, is well aware that ***hope*** postponed or delayed has the potential to make us emotionally ill. However, the less often quoted 2nd part of this verse reveals:

- He is always encouraging us to pursue the fulfillment of the longing that He has placed in our hearts.
- He wants us to experience the life that grows out of having a desire apprehended.

So, what does all this have to do with revival? EVERYTHING. God also has desires and longings just waiting to be attained. You see, God wants revival too!

The primary questions addressed in this book are:

THE CONDITIONS

> Do we know Him well enough to understand and cooperate with how He works?

HIS CHARACTER

> Do we know Him well enough to understand and cooperate with who He is?

OUR CO-LABOR

> Do we know Him well enough to understand and cooperate with who He has made us?

If you are yearning to cooperate with God and participate in His desire for a Great Awakening (a by-product of revival) then I pray this book encourages and strengthens your faith. I am writing to those who seek to properly RESPOND and be RESPONSIBLE with revival.

As you begin your journey through these pages, allow me to pray for you:

Heavenly Father, Maker of heaven and earth, of all that is seen and unseen, I pray that You will proclaim and declare over those who read this book the truth that You have recorded in Jeremiah 9:23-24:

> *This is what the Lord says:*
> *"Let not the wise boast of their wisdom*
> *or the strong boast of their strength*
> *or the rich boast of their riches,*
> *but let the one who boasts boast about this:*
> *that they* ***know and understand Me****,*
> *that I am the Lord, who exercises kindness,*
> *justice and righteousness* ***on the earth****,*
> *for in these I delight,"*
> *declares the Lord.*
>
> *—emphasis added*

In Your name I pray. Amen.

INTRODUCTION

I was on a flight to Melbourne, Florida with my pastor and dear friend, Randy Clark. One year and ten days earlier he and four members of our church in St. Louis had been asked to come and minister in Toronto, Canada. Graciously and wonderfully this small church near an airport runway was sovereignly visited by the love and power of God. Four "scheduled" days of meetings ultimately became twelve years of sustained revival in Canada that impacted millions.

Prior to our Florida trip Randy said to me, "Mark, I will know that this revival is something God wants to continue to impart if I see it happen again somewhere else besides Toronto." He explained that the area pastors in Melbourne were from various denominational and ministerial backgrounds - Baptist, Presbyterian, Vineyard, Independent Charismatic, and others. Some of these pastors had been meeting for six years to pray together and encourage unity. Randy stated, "I have a feeling that God wants to honor this type of unity. I think He is pleased with them and wants to come."

"Randy, I'm a young man and I have never seen what I would call a *REAL* MOVE OF GOD – I want to see one!" These words bolted out of my mouth. But, how had I gotten to this place where *out of my heart, my mouth spoke* these words? What had happened to produce such a request? Let's set the stage in Chapters 1 & 2.

CHAPTER 1

A Visitation of Personal and Corporate Revival:

If we would just have REAL REVIVAL!

My wife, Tammy, and I served as lay leaders with Randy Clark and the Vineyard Christian Fellowship of St. Louis, Missouri from 1990 – 1998. Our small local church experienced an influential visitation of the Holy Spirit in September of 1993. This life changing movement of God's Spirit was the catalyst for what the British media termed the Toronto Blessing beginning in January of 1994. The following December I was asked by Randy and Deanne Clark to serve as Randy's first traveling ministry partner and administrator. I did this from 1994 – 1998. This was the beginning of the ministry that is now known as Global Awakening (www.globalawakening.com). I had the privilege of ministering in our local church, throughout the United States, and in multiple countries during this time.

I am often asked what it was like in those early days. How did it start? How did God influence our local community of believers in Jesus to love Him and serve Him with a pure heart and with passion? What did it look like as we experienced the enabling power of the Holy Spirit in our various ministry activities?

To those who want to know the answer to these questions, I would like to:

1. Share how it began for me personally, and then
2. Provide a sampling of what you would have heard taught at the St. Louis Vineyard Church during that time.

My hope is that this will encourage you and give you additional insight into our overall topic of revival.

PERSONAL BEGINNINGS:

On Friday evening September 3rd 1993, Tammy and I were sitting on the couch in our living room having a very significant and real conversation. I spoke first, "Tammy, I am completely done dealing with other people's problems. I've lost my heart for people, so I guess I've lost my heart for ministry. After all, people and ministry kind of go together." Tammy looked at me compassionately and then answered me honestly. "I agree with you Mark. It is obvious that you are just going through the motions with very little passion. Ultimately you and I know that the real problem is not with the people and their issues, it's with us." So there we were left looking at each other silently, neither one having the solution.

It was good and honorable that we were taking the time to be honest, assessing and taking inventory of our spiritual condition. But let me be clear, we had absolutely no strategy, plan, or insight into how we could change the condition. We were born again, we loved God, we were faithful to the disciplines of prayer, Bible study, sharing our faith and teaching others. Neither one of us was convicted that there was any specific sin in our lives producing this condition. We simply had *grown weary in doing good.*

WEARY IN DOING GOOD:

This was the condition of our hearts as we entered Randy's office at church the next day. I had scheduled a meeting of our home group to discuss the type of activities two of the members wanted us to focus on. Days earlier I had tried to explain that I felt the activities they were suggesting would not be the most productive and best way of spending our time together as a group. Afterwards these two members spoke to individuals in the group to convince them that we needed to follow their agenda. This caused confusion and disunity. Remember, the last thing I wanted to deal with was people and problems like these.

Randy was so gracious and let these two people speak and share their thoughts. He wanted to honor them but at the same time he wanted to support Tammy and me. Rather than ask me to explain my perspective, Randy simply asked us to all join hands and pray. What happened next was unexpected and the beginning of our personal revival.

As soon as Randy asked for the Lord's presence to come and give us wisdom, I fell to my knees and began to cry. Then Tammy fell to her knees and began to cry also. We were facing one another on the floor with our foreheads touching. The following words began to flow out of my mouth –

> *"Lord I know you are telling me that the view from the top of the mountain is so much more beautiful and clear, but I do not want to climb anymore. Lord I know you are telling me that the most precious fruit is found out at the end of the branch, but I don't want to go out on a limb*

anymore, I just want to hang onto the trunk for dear life and feel safe."

I remember hearing Randy pray the following as he laid his hands on us, "A humble and contrite heart the Lord will not despise." The meeting ended with the two group members apologizing to me and Tammy and expressing their support.

Tammy and I were very quiet on our drive home. I sensed the Lord reminding me that a dear woman in our church had written us a card expressing a vision she had during her quiet time. I pull out the card and we read it again.

> *"Mark and Tammy, as I pray for you this morning I must share the beautiful image placed in my mind. You both were on your knees heads bowed before the Lord on his throne. It was a ceremony, a sending forth, if you will. He anointed your bowed heads with the trickling of warm oil starting at the crown of your heads running down the back of your necks. Then I saw you both walking side-by-side together, unafraid, with compassion and love radiating to the point that it created a protective light around you, a holy protection. You were walking with God's purpose, in His strength, without any distraction. Then I asked the Lord, "But I don't see their precious daughter?" He then brought to my mind young David who was anointed and chosen at a very young age, and then prepared and refined over time. May the Lord bless you both, God is so good!*

This card was dated September 3rd 1992 – exactly one year earlier than our conversation on the couch. Indeed, God is GOOD! His mercies endure forever and He does make ALL things beautiful in HIS time!

After my experience in Randy's office I found that I was completely renewed and again caring for others. It was a blessing and not a burden. I was revived, renewed, empowered and alive again.

Soon I found myself driving to our local church straight from work. I would go into the empty sanctuary alone and walk through every row and touch every chair praying and asking the Lord to refresh us as a people. I asked Him to be blessed by visiting us in power. I asked that He increase our love for Him. After three weeks of this Randy walked in during one of these times of prayer in the sanctuary. He said he had noticed me coming every day and wanted me to share with him what was going on. I told him the story that you just read. I told him how I'd lost my heart for people and ministry. I told him that I had no answers for my condition. I told him that God touched me in his office during that prayer. And I told him I had been revived.

I was shocked with what he said next, "Mark would you mind sharing this with our congregation this coming Sunday morning?" I told him it would be an honor. After he left I was surprised that I had agreed so quickly. After all, I had never seen anyone preach or teach on a Sunday morning in our church besides Randy up to this time.

On that following Sunday morning I shared my testimony. In addition, I found myself stating what I felt would occur in the near future of our local church. Looking back, I believe the Lord was allowing a prophecy to be spoken to all of us. I remember sharing how God was going to begin to bring people that did not look like us, talk like us, smell like us. These people were going to take our parking spots and sit in our favorite chairs. They were going to look and see if our love for God and them was real or not. And God was going to allow this in order to test our hunger and our thirst for serving others. In other words, would we welcome a movement of God the Holy Spirit if it required us to die to ourselves and our conveniences, routines and comfort zones.

I did not know that Randy was on the verge of a nervous breakdown as he sat on the front row listening to me speak that Sunday morning. His staff had been covering for him and he was in a place of great distress and potential depression. He worked hard to do what any good pastor would do, but he had been fighting the good fight in his own strength and he was losing the battle.

That Sunday night is when Randy received his famous phone call at midnight. You can read this part of the story in Randy's excellent biographical book titled, *Lighting Fires.*

CORPORATE BEGINNINGS:

Randy and our church leadership intentionally focused on promoting a biblical basis for personal and corporate revival. Although the spiritual awakening / revival our local church experienced was new to us; we knew it was not new or unusual to God or biblical Christian church history.

Following is a sampling of what you would have heard taught at the St. Louis Vineyard Church at that time. This comes directly from both the sermon notes and audio recordings of three separate Sunday morning services in June and August of 1995. Randy Clark was teaching.

From June 1995:

I have spent the last 20 years of my life trying to figure out how to best produce the values we have as a church and accomplish them. I have tried many good plans and methods. I have attempted to implement many denominational programs. I have tried everything I could that was developed by well-intentioned people. But, I have been discouraged. I have concluded that the best way to see these things happen in our church, or any church, is to experience a full blown revival. I am speaking about genuine revival. As I have been studying I have discovered that in genuine revival there is always increase. An increase in empowering with gifting and passion to reach the lost in evangelism, increase in church planting, and increase in missions. There is a God given love which changes the way we treat each other in our family relationships. There is a breaking of our hearts in prayer for our families, church, and nation; there is a rediscovery of worship, and Bible study; and there is a great burden for the hurting people of our society who need to be ministered to with acts of mercy. Only a genuine revival will accomplish this.

I want to see the ***fruits*** *of revival now. I want to see people changed at the depths of their beings. I want to see the time in our city when 100,000 to 500,000 would be saved in a brief time. I am thankful for what God has done through us these past 21 months, but I am also embarrassed by how little we have advanced. It is my desire to lead this church into a full blown Holy Ghost Revival. This is done by preaching the Word of God,* *especially addressing those things God has used in the past to bring about revival.*

<u>From August 1995</u>:
During the last few weeks we have been preaching upon the subject of "Revival". I believe this is what the Spirit is leading us to do. So, until God gives us the green light to change to another major theme - we will be bringing messages which will in some way contribute to our church moving into a full blown revival.

In the past you have heard me mention meetings in other countries where they are experiencing the fruits of revival like Argentina, China, and Korea. You have heard me mention meetings in Argentina where a lay preacher by the name of Carlos Annacondia has seen over 2 million people saved in the last 10 years. You have heard me mention the meetings held by Omar Cabrera Sr. where thousands have been healed.

Now, I know that for many of you this information and the stories and the numbers don't do a thing for you. But, let me explain why it does excite me.

First, it is what the numbers represent for me. Behind every number is a person. Someone for whom Jesus died on the Cross. Each number represents a father or a mother who was abusing or being abused; or who were in bondage to drugs or sex; or who were in bondage to demonic spirits which were destroying their lives. Each number represents teenagers who were just beginning to be destroyed by the devil, the destroyer. The numbers represent some father and husband who is destroying the very ones he loves due to his being in bondage to alcohol or drugs and often the demon power behind the addiction. The numbers represent some children who have been raised in total spiritual darkness and fear, but someone has brought them to the meetings, and they have discovered light and life in Jesus. Truly those who sat in darkness have seen a great light. You see I think of revival in these spiritual terms, where individuals are exchanging spiritual masters.

Powerful revivals do not come easy, and we need to be motivated to pray in order to release the powers of heaven to bring us victory against the powers of darkness.

For me, when I speak of revival's fruits, I also think of greater releases of healing. I know that there have been other great revivals where healings did not occur. But, I do not want to give up any ground to the enemy which we have won. For nearly 1,000 years the masses of the church have not been open to the possibility of healing occurring in the lives of the people in their churches. Only within the past 89 years has there been a much greater expectancy for healing. The Azusa Street Revival, the 1948 Healing Revival, and the Charismatic Revival, and the Vineyard Movement have emphasized healing in connection to revival. It is healing that pulls me more than anything else to press into God for revival. I am tired and emotionally disturbed by the ones who are not being healed. The little boy whose body I saw wasting away in New Jersey. The mother was looking to me with hope that their son could be released from the twisted, deteriorating body that had become their family's prison. I was troubled by the very young, the teens, and the Chinese elderly I prayed for in San Francisco for deafness. I am troubled for the mentally ill I pray for in our church and the ones I prayed for in Grand Rapids, MI. I am troubled by the blind in countless cities who come to the meetings with hope of leaving and seeing their loved ones. I think of a pretty blonde headed girl who had lost her sight when she was in kindergarten and now is about 12 years old. She had such expectation, I wanted so badly for her to see.

I am seeing many people with illnesses and diseases like the ones I just mentioned getting healed, but these numbers need to be larger. When I talk of revival, it means we will see larger numbers of individuals with the need for healing coming to us.

Perhaps one of the reasons we are not crying out for revival is that we have lost the ability to see as Jesus said that the fields are white unto harvest. You know they say that if you watch a lot of violence on the TV that you become desensitized to it, that it no longer bothers you. I believe this is true. But, I also believe that we have been watching the devil violate family, friends, and neighbors, and sadly, that no longer bothers us. We have lost our ability to feel their pain, we have lost the ability to cry over their desperation. Have we forgotten that we are to bring light into the darkness; or have we forgotten that those who need light are really out there?

Revival is exciting to me because I was saved at the beginning of a church revival. DeAnne, my wife, was saved in another church revival. I was called to preach in that same revival. My dad was saved in a church revival, and my grandpa gave his life to Jesus the same night kneeling right beside my dad. My grandpa got up from that altar of prayer and was no longer a womanizing, alcoholic who put fear in the heart of his children. He was changed by the power of God.

So when I talk about numbers I ask you to translate those figures into somebody. A father, a mother, a grandparent, a husband, a wife, or child. Some young man or woman being called into the ministry; someone being set free from the horror of addiction. We must see all of these are changed by the power of the Holy Spirit. Therefore, let us not become tired or bored or ridicule the subject of revival. Let us pray according to 2 Chronicles 7:14 and see renewal mature into revival.

IF WE (my people which are called by my name)

- *Shall humble ourselves*
- *and pray*
- *and seek His face*
- *and turn from our wicked ways*

THEN HE (I will)

- *hear from heaven*
- *will forgive our sin*
- *heal our land*

CHAPTER 2

What Revival Is NOT?

If we would just have REAL REVIVAL!

REVIVAL DEFINED:

If I were to ask an American to "Please describe my ***pants***," he would immediately look at the clothing I was wearing below my waist, to the top of my shoes. However, if I were to ask the same question to a citizen in England, they would instruct me to pull down the clothing that the American just identified in order to describe my boxers or briefs! You see the word ***pant*** refers to a completely different article of clothing depending on your place/culture/reference of origin.

This same dilemma can occur when defining the word ***revival***. Our definitions of revival may vary due to our different cultures and experiences. These differences may unintentionally create an approach to this topic that causes confusion or disunity. This could damage our ability to have valuable discussion and learn from one another. I am not insisting that you agree with all or any of my criteria for defining the word *revival.* I simply want you to know the foundational language from which I am approaching our dialogue.

The testimonies of Matthew, Mark, Luke & John clearly reveal Jesus empowering and releasing His followers to offer the "Good News." An unbiased and thorough study of these writings illustrates that this good news was demonstrated through the following:

1. Teaching
2. Healing the sick and raising the dead
3. Setting people free by casting out demons
4. Miracles of provision
5. Signs that produce awe & wonder of God

These practical, wonderful, magnificent demonstrations – as awesome as they are – must not to be confused with our need to seek and maintain personal revival.

It takes both a "revived" person and a "revived" people to authentically represent and offer the **fruits** of revival:

- Salvation
- Discipleship
- Healing
- Miracles
- Deliverance
- Signs & Wonders

However, these **fruits** of revival should not be confused with the **roots** of revival!

With this in mind, let's first discuss what revival is ***NOT.***

REVIVAL IS NOT SALVATION / CONVERSION / OR JUSTIFICATION.

When we come in faith (abiding trust) and choose to believe in and receive the person of Jesus the Christ as our Savior, and surrender to Him as Lord of our lives, we are newly born by the Holy Spirit of God. We become children of God.

We are not reviving spiritual life that we previously had; we are beginning a new spiritual life given by God for the first time.

This truth first became real to me when I was walking along the beach in Daytona, Florida at 1:00 AM. For some reason I was not tired so I went for a walk to pray. After about 20 minutes, I felt enticed to walk toward a small pier. When I got there I noticed a young man sitting under the pier leaning against the sea wall. He was looking down with a beer sitting next to him. I said, "Hello, are you doing okay?" He raised his head, looked at me, and said "Are you a Christian?" I responded, "As a matter fact I am." Without any prompting from me, he began to share how he came to Daytona Beach with a group from his college for spring break. This was the fourth day of what was intended to be a five-day week of partying. He continued, "I am absolutely miserable. Why does it feel like this?" I noticed that he began digging a hole in the sand while he talked to me. "I was just sitting here thinking about some guys I know on campus back home who are involved with a Christian group and I asked God to help me. But I don't really know what I need help for? And then you walked up to me just now."

I had the privilege of asking this young man if he wanted to know God personally and receive the help he was looking for directly from HIM. After we briefly discussed how Jesus Christ is the one who could do this for him, I asked if he would like to pray and invite Jesus to be the Savior and Lord of his life. As soon as I asked him that question, I recognized that he had placed his beer in the hole he had dug, and buried it. Then he got up on his knees and started to speak a beautiful prayer, a heartfelt prayer, and a sincere prayer – he cried out for Jesus to forgive him and come into his life. It was an honor to observe. We met the next morning for breakfast and he left to return home later that afternoon. Two weeks later I received a letter in the mail from him. He said he was now attending a great Christian group on campus and was so excited about growing in his new relationship with the Lord.

I share this story to illustrate that as wonderful and glorious as it was for God to move heaven and earth to ensure that this young man received the help he was crying out for at 1:00 AM - this magnificent, sovereign, divine appointment and life-changing event was **not** and is **not** revival. This story was an illustration of biblical Salvation / Conversion / Justification.

> *Jesus replied to him, "Truly, I tell you emphatically; unless a person is born from above he cannot see the kingdom of God." Nicodemus asked him, "How can a person be born when he is old? He can't go back into his mother's womb a second time and be born, can he?" Jesus answered, "Truly, I tell you emphatically, unless a person is born of water and Spirit he cannot enter the kingdom of God. What is born of the flesh is flesh, and what is born of the Spirit is spirit. Don't be astonished that I told you, 'All of you must be born from above.'*
>
> —JOHN 3: 3 - 7, ISV

Yet to all who did receive him, to those who believed in his name, he gave the right to become children of God—children born not of natural descent, nor of human decision or a husband's will, but born of God.

—JOHN 1: 12 - 13, NIV

BIBLICAL JUSTIFICATION

This is how our salvation/conversion is completed. At the moment of our conversion we are made righteous in God's sight – ***justification*** is the legal term for this. It means we are declared no longer guilty of the claims placed upon us by our sins. Jesus was declared guilty for us as a provision of the Father and His own willingness to pay our debt. Jesus pays the penalty for our sin that separates us from a living relationship with God. He ensures that the requirements of a righteous God are met. Justice is served in His death, burial, resurrection, and ascension.

An illustration of this truth:

You are in a courtroom standing before the judge. There is no doubt that you are guilty of the crime for which you are accused. The evidence against you is irrefutable. The gavel falls and the ruling is declared: "Guilty as charged!" The judge then explains that you can serve 6 years in jail or pay a hefty fine of $600,000 - a fine you cannot afford. Head down, sunken in despair and shaking, you cannot speak. Then the judge does something unusual. He rises to his feet, removes his robe, and steps down. Standing next to you and facing the stand he states loudly, "I choose to pay this man's fine and secure his freedom from all accusations. The only condition to my offer is that he must choose to let me." In tears you agree to the condition. He then walks with you to the court cashier and writes a check giving you the receipt for your own personal records. The receipt has the words "PAID IN FULL" stamped on it. The judge gives you a hug and says he needs to get back to court. As the two of you part you say: "Thank you Dad, I'm sorry I brought you shame today. When you get home tonight can we talk? I need you to help me change?"

The judge ruled and pronounced the legal verdict. You were not let off the hook. But then the same man stepped into his primary role in your life. He is first and foremost your father. He paid the debt you owed because he loves you. Mercy triumphed over judgment because he is first your father and then your judge. He volunteered to pay your debt and you chose to receive his offer.

Do you see? This is exactly what your Heavenly Father did when He sacrificed His son Jesus. Jesus died on the cross for your sins and for the sins of the world. He paid the penalty you owe. God is a righteous judge who pronounces you guilty and then turns around to pay your debt through the death of His Son.

If you have not yet done so, this would be a great time to express your need for the payment of your sins. You can pray like this:

<u>A prayer of gratitude and surrender</u>:

> *Heavenly Father, I thank You for giving Your only Son to die for me. Jesus, I have sinned—I have messed up. I can't make up for the things I've done wrong. As a choice of my will I ask You to forgive me. Thank You for dying on the*

cross and paying the price for me so that I can be free from the penalty of sin, guilt and shame. Thank You for doing for me what I cannot do for myself. I ask You to give me a new beginning. Take control of my life and fill me with the Holy Spirit. Make me the person You created me to be. Amen.

REVIVAL IS NOT A SUBSTITUTE FOR PERSONAL REPENTANCE AND CHRISTIAN DISCIPLESHIP.

I hope that the following stories will illustrate what I mean by the above statement.

Please note that in each of the events you are about to read the person was already a Christian (born again by the Holy Spirit) before my interactions with them.

Story 1
Personal Repentance was the Root.
Peace was the Fruit.

I was praying for a single woman in Guatemala who felt she could never live above feelings of unworthiness and shame. While interviewing her I discovered that before she knew Christ she had conceived a child with a man she loved, but they were not married. He demanded that she get an abortion or he would leave her. She carried out his request and aborted the child. He left her anyway – never to be seen again. After becoming a Christian, she recognized that she needed to truly forgive this man for what he had done. She was obedient to the Lord and sincerely forgave. However, she still battled with overwhelming emotions of worthlessness and shame. I explored further with her, "Have you ever asked the Lord to forgive you ***AND*** then forgiven yourself through Christ for the abortion?" She began to cry and stated, "I am so ashamed – I can't come to Him for myself." I gently led her in asking the Lord for His forgiveness and the power to forgive herself. I also helped her to ask the Lord to remove all past sexual and emotional attachments with the man she had conceived with. Her tears of sorrow soon turned into a humble and thankful smile of joy and peace. The Lord came upon her and her countenance changed.

By doing this she was personally repenting and asking the Lord to remove the barriers she had created through sin. She took back her responsibility to be a daily follower (disciple) of Jesus.

Story 2
Personal Repentance was the Root.
Reconnection to God was the Fruit.

I had just preached in a Southern Baptist Church when a young lady came forward to speak with me. She began to share how she felt completely distant from God and that no matter what she did she could not get close to Him. As she spoke I heard an inner voice of the Holy Spirit telling me that she was involved in a lesbian relationship and that God had been speaking to her about the need to end it. I asked her, "Do you think there is any area in your life that God has been asking you to give to Him or to change?" She immediately said, "No." I told her not to rush and asked if she was sure that there was no area that God was pointing out to her. Again, she immediately responded "*No*." I said, "Well then, if not, you should be able to draw near and hear from God." Three days later she called my wife, Tammy, and stated that she was in a lesbian relationship. She went on to say that she was currently living with the girl, and that God had been convicting her that she must move out and break it off. Tammy thanked her for being so honest, ensuring her that she was hearing from God and that she could trust Him to give her the power to obey. The girl let Tammy know that she wasn't sure if she was going to follow through. She ended communication with us.

Ten years later, during a time of worship in a completely different church, city and state, someone taps me on the shoulder. The woman asked us if I remembered her. It was the girl! She shared that she had separated from the relationship a few months after her conversation with Tammy. God had become so real and close to her after this. She was now in full-time ministry with Compassion International. Praise God!

Story 3
Personal Repentance was the Root.
Healing was the Fruit.

In Brazil, Tammy was praying for a woman who had a protruding stomach tumor. When she placed her hand on the tumor and prayed it moved from one side of the woman's stomach to the other. I joined in praying and received a word of knowledge regarding adultery. I asked the woman if her husband had committed adultery. She said, “No,” confessing that she was the one who had been unfaithful. She had broken off the adulterous relationship a year earlier, had fully confessed to her husband, and they were wonderfully reconciled. I then felt prompted to ask her if she had ever confessed and repented to the Lord for her adultery; she said "No." Tammy led her to ask the Lord to forgive her for choosing to enter into the adulterous relationship and ignoring His voice. As she finished this prayer she began to cry and groan. She fell to the floor as we commanded the tumor to leave and it shrank and disappeared.

BIBLICAL SANCTIFICATION

Sanctification is a process. Our journey to wholeness takes time as we allow the Spirit of God to apply the good news of the gospel to every area of our life. Many of us have not grown, matured, or defeated sinful structures in our lives because we have not committed to personal repentance and on-going discipleship.

When we commit to becoming followers / disciples of Jesus and give Him continual lordship in our lives, we are seeking to mature by the Holy Spirit of God. As we apply the biblical principle of personal repentance we ask the Lord to remove the barriers we have created through our sin. We choose to abide in Jesus, remaining a daily follower. This process is known as ***sanctification***.

New Testament salvation, which includes both justification and sanctification, is immediate and continuing. It has the component of process - we are, and continue to be, saved!

When we are born again some aspects of our lives change with our willful cooperation. Other areas change without us noticing a difference until later. Regardless of how the changes transpire, we still have a personal responsibility to pursue and follow the Lord daily. Biblical sanctification is our pathway to maturity and fullness in Christ.

There are portions of our being that have yet to submit to the good news of salvation, thus these parts of our lives still need to appropriate what has already been accomplished by the death and resurrection of Jesus. Full salvation is found in Christ and His work on the cross. The blood shed by Jesus, the Lamb of God, washes away guilt. His forgiveness frees us from condemnation. His cross crucifies sin structures in our lives. He became a curse for us, and breaks the power of curses. His resurrection life restores our life. His acceptance welcomes and restores our soul. His gentle touch, ministered by the Holy Spirit, brings healing to wounds that remain under the surface of our lives. We discover what it means to have the Kingdom of God prominent within us.

A Christian's ability to repent (change their wrong thinking, attitudes and actions) is reliant on a power source outside themselves. This resource is God given and is now made available to all of us who believe in the atoning work of Jesus Christ.

> *..., From that time Jesus began to preach and to say, "Repent, for (presents the cause or gives the reason of a preceding statement) the kingdom of heaven is at hand."*
>
> — MATTHEW 4:17, NKJV

> *..., and saying, "The time is fulfilled, and the kingdom of God is at hand. Repent, and believe in the gospel."*
>
> — MARK 1:16, NKJV

In Other Words:

> Now is the time, change your thinking, attitudes and actions because a new resource is now available and is within your reach to obtain and make use of – ***The Kingdom of God***[1]

This involves our cooperation with the third person of the trinity/Godhead - the Holy Spirit. We have a responsibility to present ourselves to God by committing to being a follower/disciple. We must seek to renew our minds, walking in the reality that we are no longer enslaved to sinful attitudes and actions. By seeking the power of the Holy Spirit we grow in our capacity to live with God and for God. We learn that:

Personal Relationship with God is the Root. ***Power to Obey God is the Fruit.***

> *But solid food is for mature people, whose minds are trained by practice to distinguish good from evil.*
>
> —HEBREWS 5: 14, INTERNATIONAL STANDARD VERSION

> *To him who is able to keep you from stumbling and to present you before his glorious presence without fault and with great joy — to the only God our Savior....*
>
> —JUDE 1: 24 – 25B, NIV

REVIVAL IS NOT PHYSICAL HEALING / DELIVERANCE / OR SIGNS & WONDERS

"Physically I'm doing very well, but you have to pray for me and my husband. It seems like were fighting and bickering all the time!"

I could not believe what I was hearing on the other end of this phone call. I was talking to a dear woman who had received a creative miracle. Three months earlier we had been in Hendersonville Tennessee and after prayer she was healed of Atypical Idiopathic Parkinson's disease. She came forward that night for prayer with her husband. She weighed approximately 85 pounds, could not walk unassisted and was shaking. That evening after prayer all the shaking stopped. She walked up unassisted to the stage and began to play the keyboard. We were all in tears as she played the old gospel hymn, "He Touched Me."

Then the hand of Jesus touched me,
And now I am no longer the same.

He touched me, O, He touched me,
And O, the joy that floods my soul.
Something happened, and now I know,
He touched me and made me whole.

Since I met this blessed Savior,
Since He cleansed and made me whole;
I will never cease to praise Him,
I'll shout it while eternity rolls.

She and her husband shared with us how years earlier she was playing the piano on a stage prior to her husband preaching in an evangelistic meeting. Suddenly her mind went blank, she could not play and she ran off the stage in embarrassment. Soon after this she received her diagnosis. Upon further testing it was discovered that she had lost, and was continuing to lose, function within her brain due to this cruel disease.

At the beginning of our phone call this precious lady joyfully told me that she had gained 25 pounds, was able to drive again, was holding her grandchildren safely without shaking for the first time in years, was doing laundry and was back to cooking meals. She was grocery shopping and playing the piano again as well.

Perhaps now you can understand my confusion when she said that I had to pray for their marriage. Upon further questioning, this is what I discovered:

Due to the poor physical condition she had been in for years, her husband had become the full-time chauffeur, homemaker, and caretaker of their home. He oversaw their social calendar and made the decisions as to what each day's schedule would be. He had developed and maintained the routine of their home. But now, as wonderful as this healing had been for his dear wife (and him), it was creating a new chaos of change. He was impatient, frustrated and confused about how to let his wife have her own opinions and make her own decisions. She was choosing different grocery items, she was doing the laundry her own way, she drove her own routes, and she had the strength to argue and express herself. She was recalling memories of things he had done both good and not so good and she used these memories for ammunition when they had their "discussions".

Prior to hanging up the phone I promised her I would be praying for them! When this call ended I walked into our church sanctuary and sat down in a chair. I was perplexed. I had never considered that receiving a creative miracle and wonderful physical healing could possibly bring out issues that led to difficulty. These new issues would require repentance, forgiveness, understanding, ongoing trust and surrender to the Lord. This dumbfounded me until I realized that receiving a physical healing, or as in this case a creative miracle, is not a substitute or replacement for needing daily personal revival. We still must walk in the power of the Holy Spirit and continue to follow Jesus.

Now that we have discussed what revival is ***not,*** let's continue and look at a working definition of what revival ***is***.

CHAPTER 3

What Is Revival?

If we would just have REAL REVIVAL!

<u>REVIVAL IS THE RECOVERY OF SPIRITED LIFE FROM A STATE OF NEGLECT, LETHARGY, PENDING DEATH OR APPARENT DEATH.</u>

Continuing our attempt to create a mutual definition of revival, we should ponder the following excerpts from <u>*What Is A Revival*</u> by Charles Haddon Spurgeon.[1]

C.H. Spurgeon (1834-92) was a preacher in England during most of the second half of the nineteenth century. In 1854, just four years after his conversion, Spurgeon, then only age 20, became pastor of London's famed New Park Street Church. The congregation quickly outgrew their building, moved to Exeter Hall, then to Surrey Music Hall. In these venues Spurgeon frequently preached to audiences numbering more than 10,000. In 1861 the congregation moved permanently to the newly constructed Metropolitan Tabernacle.

Regarding revival, he states:

> The word "revival" is as familiar in our mouths as any household word. We are constantly speaking about and praying for a "revival." The

word "revive" may be interpreted —to live again, to receive again a life which has almost expired; to rekindle into a flame the vital spark which was nearly extinguished.

When a person has been dragged out of a pond nearly drowned, the bystanders are afraid that he is dead, and are anxious to ascertain if life still lingers. The proper means are used to restore animation; the body is rubbed, stimulants are administered, and if by God's providence life still tarries, the rescued man opens his eyes, sits up, and speaks, and those around him rejoice that he has revived.

Those who have no spiritual life are not, and cannot be, in the strictest sense of the term, the subjects of a revival. Many blessings may come to the unconverted in consequence of a revival among Christians, but the revival itself has to do only with those who already possess spiritual life. There must be vitality in some degree before there can be a quickening of vitality, or, in other words, a revival.

A true revival is to be looked for in the church of God. Only in the river of gracious life can the pearl of revival be found. The results of the revival will extend to the outside world, but the revival, strictly speaking, must be within the circle of life of vital godliness and by them only.

It is a sorrowful fact that many, who are spiritually alive, greatly need reviving. They ought not always to be crying, "my leanness, my leanness, woe unto me." Sustained by gracious promises and enriched out of the fullness which God has treasured up in his dear Son, their souls should prosper and be in health, and their piety ought to need no reviving. They should aspire to a higher blessing, a richer mercy, than a mere revival. They have the nether springs already; they should earnestly cover the upper springs. They should be asking for growth in grace, for increase of strength, for greater success; they should have out-climbed and out-soared the period in which they need to be constantly crying, "Wilt thou not revive us again?"

For a church to be constantly needing revival is the indication of much sin, for if it were sound before the Lord it would remain in the condition into which a revival would uplift its members. A church should be a camp of soldiers, not a hospital for invalids. But there is exceedingly much difference between what ought to be and what is, and consequently many of God's people are in so sad a state that the very fittest prayer for them is for revival.

When revival comes to a people who are in the state thus briefly described, it simply brings them to the condition in which they ought always to have been; it quickens them, stirs the coals of the expiring fire, and puts heavenly breath into the languid lungs. The sickly soul which before was insensible, weak, and sorrowful, grows earnest, vigorous, and happy in the Lord.... The Holy Spirit must come into the living heart through living truth, and so bring nutriment and stimulant to the pining spirit, for so only can it be revived.

This, then, leads us to the conclusion that if we are to obtain a revival we must go directly to the Holy Spirit for it, and not resort to the machinery of the professional revival-maker. The true vital spark of heavenly flame comes from the Holy Spirit. There is no spiritual vitality in anything except as the Holy Spirit is all in all in the work; and if our vitality has fallen near to zero, we can only have it renewed by him who first kindled it in us. The Holy Spirit will recruit our strength and give us a revival.

While a true revival in its essence belongs only to God's people, it always brings with it a blessing for the other sheep who are not yet of the fold. Let the Lord revive a believer and very soon his families, his friends, his neighbors, receive a share of the benefit. When Christians are revived they live more consistently, they make their homes more holy and happier. Let us pledge ourselves to form a prayer-union, a sacred band of suppliants, and may God do unto us according to our faith.

Yes and Amen Mr. Spurgeon! Additionally it would be helpful to consider what the writers at GotQuestions.org state regarding revival [2]

Revival refers to a spiritual reawakening from a state of dormancy or stagnation in the life of a believer. It encompasses the resurfacing of a love for God, an appreciation of God's holiness, a passion for His Word and His church, a convicting awareness of personal and corporate sin, a spirit of humility, and a desire for repentance and growth in righteousness. Revival invigorates and sometimes deepens a believer's faith, opening his or her eyes to the truth in a fresh, new way. It generally involves the connotation of a fresh start with a clean slate, marking a new beginning of a life lived in obedience to God. Revival breaks the charm and power of the world, which blinds the eyes of men, and generates both the will and power to live in the world but not of the world.

Revival, in many respects, replicates the believer's experience when he or she is saved. It is initiated by a prompting of the Holy Spirit, creating an awareness of something missing or wrong in the believer's life that can only be righted by God. In turn, the Christian must respond from the heart, acknowledging his or her need. Then, in a powerful way, the Holy Spirit draws back the veil the world has cast over the truth, allowing the believers to fully see themselves in comparison to God's majesty and holiness. Obviously, such comparisons bring great humility, but also great awe of God and His truly amazing grace (Isaiah 6:5). Unlike the original conversion experience that brings about a new relationship to God, however, revival represents a restoration of fellowship with God, the relationship having been retained even though the believer had pulled away for a time.

God, through His Holy Spirit, calls us to revival in a number of situations. Christ's letters to the seven churches reveal some circumstances that may necessitate revival. In the letter to Ephesus, Christ praised the church for their perseverance and discernment, but He stated that they had forsaken their first love (Revelation 2:4-5). Many times as the excitement of acceptance to Christ grows cold, we lose the zeal that we had at first. We become bogged down in the ritual, going through the motions, but we no longer experience the joy of serving Christ. Revival helps restore that first love and passion for Christ. The cares and worries of life can beat us down, leaving us emotionally, physically, and spiritually exhausted. Revival can lift us up to new hope and faith.

CHAPTER 4

Tantalizing or Transforming

If we would just have REAL REVIVAL!

ONLY ONE FOUNDATION:

> *For no one can lay any foundation other than the one already laid, which is Jesus Christ.*
>
> —1 CORINTHIANS 3: 11, NEW INTERNATIONAL VERSION

We were ministering in Guatemala. Approximately 5,000 had gathered in a tent that reminded me of the massive circus tent I had seen as a child. The stage was very large, the tent poles extremely tall and strong. Wooden folding chairs were everywhere the eye could see, an ocean of chairs. The lighting was so well done that it felt like the middle of the day at 8:00 PM.

My pastor, Randy Clark, was next to the stage on one side of the tent and I was on the other side. People had formed a line on both sides from front to back to receive prayer from us. Without any hesitation I can tell you I have never seen more quantity of healings take place as I did here. It was beyond wonderful!

However, during one brief moment as I took a sip of water before continuing to pray, I caught a glimpse of just how many people were lined up on both sides wanting individual prayer from Randy or myself. Suddenly, the only way I know how to describe it was I felt the heart of the Holy Spirit grieved that the people were looking to Randy and I more than to God Himself. I immediately excused myself from the person I was about to pray for and went across the tent to Randy. While he was still praying I whispered in his ear what I was sensing. I could tell this was causing him to have to switch gears. He had just seen a baby that had been born blind receive vision. At this very moment the family's doctor was there with the parents and was testing the baby's eyes and confirming the healing. So it goes without saying that Randy and the family and those near us were in pure unadulterated excitement. This was the environment that Randy now had to weigh what I had whispered to him. In true humility he immediately got up on the stage took the microphone and stated that God wanted us all to ensure that we were looking to Him and not to men. He went on to say that we were all going to return to our chairs and worship for 15 minutes and that God was going to break out with spontaneous healing as we worshiped to confirm WHO the source of our healing is from.

As the music began I remember being on the steps of the stage in a kneeling position just weeping and asking the Holy Spirit not to be grieved. Thanking Him for His guidance and correction and asking Him to know we were sorry and how much we loved Him. During that 15 minutes well over 500 people were healed and spontaneously came forward closer to the stage to worship. The dear pastor of this tent church witnessed a woman directly in front of him experience her back cracking and adjusting as it became totally straight. She had just been healed of spinal scoliosis.

TANTALIZING OR TRANSFORMING:

> ***Tantalizing*** is defined as: *having or exhibiting something that provokes or arouses expectation, interest, or desire, especially that which remains unobtainable or beyond one's reach*
>
> ***Transforming*** is defined as: *to change in form, appearance, and/or structure; metamorphose; to change in condition, nature, or character; convert; to change into another substance; transmute.*

I share the previous story to illustrate that while witnessing and experiencing miracles, healings, signs and wonders can encourage and strengthen our faith, they in and of themselves have no ability to be the foundation of changing our lives. They are Divine, but they are not Discipleship. They are Wonderful, but they are not our Walk. They are Tantalizing, but they are not to be confused with our call to Transform (Romans 12: 1-2). We are to be led by the Spirit of God; not the good gifts of God.

BEFORE WE PRAY FOR CORPORATE REVIVAL

Before we pray for God to bring us revival, we must all ask ourselves this crucial question:

WHY WOULD GOD WANT TO MULTIPLY UNHEALTHINESS?

- What would others receive if God duplicated the current condition of our individual lives into them?

- What would others receive if God duplicated the current condition of our marriages into their unions?
- What would others receive if God duplicated the condition of our family into their family?
- What would others receive if God duplicated the condition of our local church into their community of faith?

RESPONSIBLE REPRODUCTION & THE HEART OF GOD

When we pray for God to bring us the lost, the addicted, the angry, the depressed, the unloved, the lonely, and the bound – do we consider what God is bringing them to? If He answers our prayers while we continue to choose living in the very same disarray they are in – He risks reproducing all of our corruptness. Why would a wise Heavenly Father, the Great Shepherd, bring them to us?

These questions remind me of an interview with evangelist Carlos Annacondia of Argentina. The history of his ministry began in May of 1979 in the city of San Justo, Buenos Aires when Carlos and his wife Maria gave their lives to Christ. The following year Carlos began to preach in poor villages of Buenos Aires and God started to perform beautiful miracles and deliverances.

During the interview we asked him,

> *"Carlos, why is it that 80% of the people that come to Christ in your crusades are still active in their local churches five years after their decision? In the U.S. large evangelistic crusades*

only retain anywhere from 2 to 4% in their churches after five years?"

Without hesitating he replied,

> *"Oh, in the USA you are very good at getting them forgiven, but you're not very good at getting them free. So, after one month or six months or a year of trying to live the Christian life and honestly being unable, their only conclusion is that they must give up, or they don't know the Lord, or they simply continue to carry a sense of guilt and shame that keeps them fruitless. You see, they are still in bondage and unable to grow or mature."*

I felt like I had been stabbed directly in the heart when I heard Carlos' response. All I can say is that from that point on I could never look at the ministry of inner healing, freedom and deliverance as peripheral to the gospel. I was confronted with an insight that required my pursuit. From that interview I knew that my excuses, and at times the excuses of the church in general, regarding the need for applying freedom ministry to those we disciple in Christ were hindering maturity and growth. Excuses such as lack of information, fears of abuse, and self-protecting doctrine were preventing myself, my family and my brothers and sisters in Christ from walking in the fullness that God had already provided.

> *For in Christ all the fullness of the Deity lives in bodily form, and in Christ you have been brought to fullness. He is the head over every power and authority.*
>
> —COLOSSIANS 2:9-10, NIV

My blinders were taken off during that interview. I saw the white fields of need and that evening I humbly confessed my inability to do this kind of kingdom freedom ministry. I specifically asked God, the Holy Spirit to grow me up and teach me.

This event led my wife, Tammy, and I to found Hand of Jesus Ministries. We have surrendered our lives to serve others in this area of gaining complete freedom.

Again, we must ask ourselves: *Why would God want to multiply unhealthiness?* If we as individuals, families, and as the corporate church are still in desperate need of freedom from darkness and its fruits – then we possess no power to bring the lost to a place of freedom, light and His fruits.

When we commit to pursuing God-given wholeness and give God permission, through repentance, to remove ungodly hooks in us – then the Lord will have a place He can wisely and caringly bring the lost.

He will have a place where spiritual health and faith can be multiplied, rather than spiritual sickness and distrust.

> *May the God of peace Himself make you holy in every way. And may your whole being—spirit, soul, and body—remain blameless when our Lord Jesus, the Messiah, appears.*
>
> — 1 THESSALONIANS 5:23, ISV

INDIVIDUAL FREE-WILL

Each of us must engage our free-will when requesting the Holy Spirit to search our lives. We ask Him to reveal, heal, remove and/or change all sinful structures that have been built into our hearts over a lifetime. By participating with Him through repentance, these sinful structures can be brought to death. They no longer produce an evil and unbelieving heart.

> *"We destroy arguments and every lofty opinion raised against the knowledge of God, and take every thought captive to obey Christ."*
>
> — 2 CORINTHIANS 10:5, ESV

It is our God given free-will which gives permission for either God and good, or Satan and evil, to work in our lives. According to 1 Thessalonians 5:23, our Spirit, our Soul (mind, will and emotions) and our Body require transformation because they are the gateway and highway for good or evil. Good attachments lead to freedom. Evil attachments lead to bondage. Our wills are utterly free to decide what attachments we invite or allow.

Whenever we see evil and wrong in the world, we can know that someone, somewhere, at some time, gave Satan's kingdom permission to work. And every time we see something of great goodness, we can know that someone, somewhere, at some time, surrendered to God and He moved in power.

God has given us His authority to shut down the works of Satan when we apply the power of the cross through repentance. The following prayer is provided as an example:

"God, I continually see (anger, addiction, fear, …) negatively effecting my life. I ask You to forgive me for (Cursing, pornography, not trusting You, …), I choose to repent. I renounce my desire and willful agreement with (anger, addiction, fear, …). I ask you to place the Cross of Jesus Christ between me and my sin. I choose to close all areas of access for these to operate and remain attached to me. I choose to reopen my Spirit, Soul and Body to You only as my Lord. Please come and fulfill Your will in my life and these situations. In the Name of Jesus I pray - Amen."

- Choosing to repent is our responsibility.

- Leading us into truth and revealing any required steps of obedience is the Holy Spirit's responsibility.

MULTIPLICATION IS SUPERIOR TO ADDITION

Perhaps you have heard the adage "The whole is only as good as the sum of its parts."

The Bible states it this way,

For just as each of us has one body with many members, and these members do not all have the same function, so in Christ we, though many, form one body, and each member belongs to all the others. We have different gifts, according to the grace given to each of us.

— ROMANS 12:4-6A

Just as a body, though one, has many parts, but all its many parts form one body, so it is with Christ. For we were all baptized by one Spirit so as to form one body—whether Jews or Gentiles, slave or free—and we were all given the one Spirit to drink. Even so the body is not made up of one part but of many.... Now you are the body of Christ, and each one of you is a part of it.

— 1 CORINTHIANS 12:12-14, 27

A real and true corporate revival can only happen when a revived person (or persons) commits to co-labor with God. Raising our level of cooperating with God as He manifests doesn't just happen as we are gathered together in the same place and at the same time. It requires the revived to influence the overall spiritual environment.

As more revived individuals surrender and submit together in an interrelated manner, this increases each other's abilities and improves each other's character and gifting. The result is the ability to multiply something greater together than the mere attempts of one or a few.

In Matthew 21:43 we are directly confronted with a warning. Jesus states clearly **why** we as his followers must pursue the cleansing, the refining, the wholeness, the realness, and the change that revival provides.

> *Therefore I tell you, the kingdom of God will be taken away from you and given to a people producing its fruits.*

We each must intentionally and consistently pursue maintaining the fruits of our personal and corporate revival experiences. Only then can we authentically represent and offer the fruits of the kingdom of God to others.

> *As you go, proclaim this message: "The kingdom of heaven has come near."*
>
> —MATTHEW 10:7

I hope you found this chapter helpful or at least thought provoking. In our next chapter we are going to move forward and consider God's perspective on revival and the conditions and consequences it creates.

CHAPTER 5

Revival: The Conditions & Consequences Created

If we would just have REAL REVIVAL!

<u>A PROFOUND QUESTION:</u>

After the first week of meetings in Melbourne, Florida it was apparent to all present that God was moving in gracious revival again. Praise His goodness towards all of us!

Randy and I needed to return to St. Louis for the weekend and then we would return to Florida the following Tuesday.

While at home I received a phone call from a friend that I had not spoken to in 5 years. Rather than catching me up on himself and his family, he immediately asked me this question:

> *"Mark, why doesn't God let out all the stops and release a flood of undeniable, in your face, healings, miracles, signs & wonders in order that the entire world would be forced to recognize He is God and there is no other?*

I could tell by the tone in his voice that he was desperate. He longed for God to be known and obtainable before all. He had reached the end of his own strength and was crying out.

When someone is in this posture, asking these types of heart-rending questions, general suggestions or wide-ranging pastoral ponderings won't do. No, the man on the other side of this phone call needed God, his Father's voice and counsel. This was a man whose heart was fragile, tender and in need. I avoided attempts to answer for God – I simply prayed for him.

I had no idea that God would speak to me through scripture the next morning in my quiet time. I was stunned to sense Him say, "*What you've just read is the answer to your friend's question.*" Want to know what I read? I thought you might!

REVIVAL CONDITIONS:

The Conditions Created

JOHN 15: 22, 24A

> *22 "**If I had not come and spoken to them**, they would not be guilty of sin; **but now** they have no excuse for their sin. 24a **If I had not done among them the works** no one else did, they would not be guilty of sin. As it is, **they have seen, and yet** they have hated both me and my Father."*

MATTHEW 11: 20-24

> *20 Then Jesus began to denounce **the towns in which most of his miracles had been performed,** because they did not repent. 21 "Woe to you, Chorazin! Woe to you, Bethsaida! For **if the***

***miracles that were performed in you** had been performed in Tyre and Sidon, they would have repented long ago in sackcloth and ashes. 22 But I tell you, it will be more bearable for Tyre and Sidon on the day of judgment than for you. 23 And you, Capernaum, will you be lifted to the heavens? No, you will go down to Hades. For **if the miracles that were performed in you** had been performed in Sodom, it would have remained to this day. 24 But I tell you that it will be more bearable for Sodom on the day of judgment **than for you**."*

JOHN 12: 47-50

*47 "**If anyone hears my words** but does not keep them, I do not judge that person. For I did not come to judge the world, but to save the world. 48 **There is a judge for the one who rejects me and does not accept my words; the very words I have spoken will condemn them at the last day**. 49 For I did not speak on my own, but the Father who sent me commanded me to say all that I have spoken. 50 I know that his command leads to eternal life. So whatever I say is just what the Father has told me to say."*

JOHN 12: 37

*37 **Even after Jesus had** performed so many signs in their presence, **they still would not believe** in him.*

JOHN 9: 39 - 41

39 Jesus said, "For judgment I have come into this world, so that the blind will see and those who see will become blind." 40 Some Pharisees who were with him heard him say this and asked,

> *"What? Are we blind too?" 41 Jesus said, "**If you were blind, you would not be guilty of sin; but now that you claim you can see, your guilt remains**.*

<u>The Consequences Created</u>

As I continued in my quiet time that morning I began to ask God about the words I was reading. How did this relate to my friend's question?

> *"Mark, why doesn't God let out all the stops and release a flood of undeniable, in your face, healings, miracles, signs & wonders in order that the entire world would be forced to recognize He is God and there is no other?*

I felt as though God was speaking to me:

> *"When I anoint the words of truth spoken AND I increase the regularity and quality of visible miracles – I am allowing increase in the corresponding level of accountability and judgment upon those present. Prior to the words spoken, they had not heard and they were not accountable. Prior to witnessing the miracles, they had not seen and were not accountable. An environment where they hear My Words and see My Works is a place of raised accountability and judgement. They will become responsible to respond to that which I am asking of them in that time."*

Further Study

"Be like a Berean!" This popular motto in many Christian congregations derives its meaning from the Book of Acts, chapter 17:10-11.

> *..., the believers sent Paul and Silas away to Berea. On arriving there, they went to the Jewish synagogue. Now the Berean Jews were of more noble character than those in Thessalonica, for* ***they received the message with great eagerness and examined the Scriptures every day to see if what Paul said was true***.

We see that the Berean Jews:

- Received the message/teaching of Paul & Silas with eagerness / readiness
- Searched the Scriptures daily to examine and consider what was being proposed

What is the word "Scriptures" referring to here? Christians today would answer "The Bible" without giving it a second thought. What we might fail to remember is that the New Testament was not available in the early 1st Century. What "Scripture" meant to Jesus, His apostles and everyone in the 1st Century, including the Bereans was – the Old Testament writings. So the Bereans were checking Paul and Silas' claims of the Good News by comparing them to the Old Testament and reviewing all the prophecies that Jesus fulfilled.

How does this relate to our discussion? We have an obligation to study what scripture says regarding Revival.

Are the conditions & consequences created consistent with and reflected in both the Old and the New Testaments?

With this in mind, let's consider…

A Not So Top Ten List:

1. Shammua
2. Shaphat
3. Igal
4. Palti
5. Gaddiel
6. Gaddi
7. Ammiel
8. Sethur
9. Nahbi
10. Geuel

Chances are you have never chosen to memorize this list of names from Numbers chapter 13. I am mentioning them because the actions of these men influenced an entire nation. My purpose in pointing them out is to emphasize the importance they represent to our topic. The unbelief of these men and the environment they created is stated in the following:

> *And the Lord said to Moses,* ***"How long will this people despise me? And how long will they not believe in me, in spite of all the signs that I have done among them?****...But truly, as I live, and as all the earth shall be filled with the glory of the Lord,* ***none of the men who have seen my glory and my signs that I did in Egypt and in the wilderness, and yet have put me to the test these ten times and have not obeyed my voice, shall see the land that I swore to give to their fathers. And none of those who despised me shall see it.***
>
> — NUMBERS 14:11 AND 21 – 23 ESV

We see God ask:

- How long will this people despise me?
- How long will they not believe in me?

What "people" is God referring to here?

- Those who had heard and seen His glory and His signs among them!

COMPELLED BY HIS PERSPECTIVE

On the basis of:

- The phone call and question I was asked by my friend AND
- My time in the book of John the following morning AND
- My sense of the Lord saying, "*What you've just read is the answer to this man's question.*" AND
- My further studies and prayer in light of both the Old and New Testaments

I began to sense a compelling obligation to recognize movements of God from ***HIS PERSPECTIVE.***

1. His words of life spoken to those who do not keep them – may judge them!
2. His miracles accomplished before those who do not repent – may condemn them!

Now my prayer became like Moses:

If you are pleased with me, teach me your ways so I may know you and continue to find favor with you. Remember that this nation is your people.'

— EXODUS 33:13, NIVUK

I propose that God wants us to discern:

> Individual and corporate accountability is to be expected when God's words and God's miracles are present.
>
> Environments experiencing His manifest presence and the accompanying increase in anointing on the words of His truth being spoken (preached / taught / communicated) and on the power displayed of His miraculous acts (healings / miracles / signs / wonders / deliverances) – creates responsibility
>
> Saying "No" or choosing to walk away from our required individual or corporate response to God has consequences that were not present prior to hearing and seeing!
>
> If we do not respond appropriately at these times, the heart of God the Father is grieved, however He is obligated to always act out of who HE IS – a righteous judge!

<u>His Character and His Concern</u> - this is what we are going to examine in the following chapter.

CHAPTER 6

His Character & His Concern

If we would just have REAL REVIVAL!

WHO HE IS:

After my quiet time that morning, I chose to study further. I wanted additional insight regarding how God's character (who He is) is PARAMOUNT to ***real revival.***

His Character

Then the Lord came down in the cloud and stood there with him and proclaimed his name, the Lord. And he passed in front of Moses, proclaiming, 'The Lord, the Lord, the compassionate and gracious God, slow to anger, longsuffering, abounding in love and faithfulness, maintaining love to thousands, and forgiving wickedness, rebellion and sin. Yet he does not leave the guilty unpunished...

— EXODUS 34:5-7A ESV

The Lord is longsuffering and abundant in mercy, forgiving iniquity and transgression; but He by no means clears the guilty ...

— NUMBERS 14:18A

What if God, wanting to show His wrath and to make His power known, endured with much longsuffering the vessels of wrath prepared for destruction...

— Romans 9:22

The Lord is not slack concerning His promise, as some count slackness, but is longsuffering toward us, not willing that any should perish but that all should come to repentance.... and consider that the longsuffering of our Lord is salvation —....

— 2 Peter 3:9 & 15a

What character trait of God do you notice most in the scriptures you just read?

<u>Longsuffering</u>

- The New Testament Greek word = *makrothumia.*
- Root Words = *Makro*, meaning "long," and *Thumos*, meaning "temper."
- A Literal reading is:

  To be long-tempered. Holding back a long time before expressing judgment in passionate words and/or actions.
- When scripture says that God **<u>IS</u>** longsuffering this is more than describing His behavior. It is defining His Character. It is stating who He is, not simply what He does. He **<u>IS</u>** longsuffering!
- Longsuffering is a Fruit of the Holy Spirit and thus dwells in the spirit of Christian believers.

His Concern

Do you sense the tension here? Do you feel the conflict that God so wisely and caringly has to balance? The Lord hears every prayer of his precious children. He stores in heaven our cries for His glory to visit us. Yet this dear precious Lord must be the Master of balanced measures. He must judicially orchestrate the apparent conditions of impasse.

- ***He desires*** to releases a move of His Holy Spirit in response to the prayer of His people.
- ***He knows*** the potential for harm for those who hear and see if they are not prepared to respond appropriately.

God desires to gather us under his protective wings, but He knows that many of us are not prepared to let Him. He desires ALL to come to repentance – while being aware that NOT ALL will. His heart breaks when we refuse His offer of relationship.

Only God knows when a person, a family, a church, a city, or a nation is prepared to be brought to a greater level of accountability and potential judgment. He manages the timing of outpourings and greater anointing. He coordinates the activities of awakenings, all the while being constrained by the longsuffering love of who He is.

I greatly appreciate how Bill Johnson, pastor of Bethel church in Redding California, expresses this same concept. He states, [1]

In the introduction to the parable of the seed and the sower we find that Jesus did not merely use parables as illustrations, but at times to conceal truth so that only the hungry would understand (See Matt. 13:11, 18-23). It is the mercy of God to withhold revelation from those who have no hunger for truth; because if they don't hunger for it, the chances are they won't obey it when they hear it. Revelation always brings responsibility, and hunger is the thing that prepares our hearts to carry the weight of that responsibility. By keeping revelation from those without hunger, God actually protects them from certain failure to carry the responsibility it would lay on them.

What is it that God wants us to understand and know about His ways? How do we cooperate with Him and His desire for revival?

CHAPTER 7

Our Co-Labor: Changing Perspective

If we would just have REAL REVIVAL!

THE REVIVAL EQUATION

> *If you are pleased with me, teach me your ways so I may know you and continue to find favour with you. Remember that this nation is your people.'*
>
> — EXODUS 33:13, NIVUK

> *.... How often I wanted to gather your children together, as a hen gathers her brood under her wings, but you were not willing!*
>
> — LUKE 13:34

REVIVAL:

God has revealed the **Conditions & Consequences Created** (Chapter 3)

God has revealed **His Character & Concern** (Chapter 4)

=

God knows the perfect time that a person, a family, a church, a city, a village, or a nation is prepared.

ARE WE SEEING FROM GOD'S PERSPECTIVE?

It was 1994 when I began to carry within me the equation above. I was grateful for His wisdom. I was also indebted to Him for allowing me to know His character and His care. But, I did not know what to do with the information He had given.

Sometime around 2004 I realized that I had unintentionally ended my journey. I found myself applying a definition of God's sovereignty that was counterproductive and in conflict with God's purposes. My reasoning went something like this:

I saw no alternative except to wait on God to send His outpourings. He is the only one who knows the condition of every man, woman and child's heart. He is the only one who knows when the soil is prepared to hear and see "greater things." So I found myself inactively waiting for Him to initiate and move in His "perfect" timing

I lived in a world that required no faith on my part. I simply did my best to love and care for others. If God "chose" to move in power that was His prerogative. Increased outpouring may or may not happen. I could never know if people's hearts (and mine) were prepared enough for God to safely release an increase of His presence in greater power. I decided it was all up to Him. I felt no responsibility on my part.

But praise God that He saw my child-like ignorance! He knew I was inappropriately applying an incorrect definition of His sovereignty. He graciously continued to teach me His ways.

THE JOURNEY CONTINUES

Permit me to ask you two specific questions.

Question 1:

> Would you agree that we cannot change **GOD'S CHARACTER**?

I am going to assume that your answer to this question is, "**YES!**" You are convinced that we are not responsible to try and change who God is. In fact, the question seems ridiculous to you (and me too!).

Question 2:

> Would you agree that we cannot change **THE CONDITIONS** needed for an outpouring of His presence?

I will not assume your answer to this question.

I used to believe that I could not effect the conditions. I now believe it is my responsibility as a Christian to co-labor with God. I also believe it is OUR shared responsibility as His Church to change conditions.

Allow me to explain:

OUR CO-LABOR AND A PROPOSITION

What does co-laboring look like?

Here is an Old Testament example from 2 Samuel Chapter 21.

V. 1 <u>During the reign of David</u>, there was a famine for three successive years; so David sought the face of the LORD.

God's perspective is shown in the first five words of this verse: this occurred in the place and time of David's "reign".

Let's look at the CONDITIONS and David's perspective: There was a prolonged famine during this time and it occurred in the place/location of David's reign. David perceives that he has God's favor and God's delegated authority. This is important to note because "we also" are to reign over the issues of our lives. We too have God's delegated authority. He calls us to "reign" through Him.

David considers the circumstances, he ponders and concludes that such prolonged lack, loss, and want is NOT characteristic of His God. He insists that such on-going lack of provision is not of God. Therefore, David takes action. He doesn't call in the elders. He doesn't form a financial committee. He doesn't demand that others assume his responsibility of reign. Instead David chooses to seek his God (our God) for specific answers. David committed himself to seeing the situation change. He needs insight into the cause of this famine and he expects to get it. David has concluded that such prolonged lack is not consistent with who he knows God to be.

It would serve us well to pause and ask:

1. Do I have the same perspective over my life as God has?

2. Do I see myself as having His reign over my own life?
3. Am I taking responsibility to seek the counsel of God?
4. Have I thrown away all my expectations of experiencing a life lived ***with*** Him?
5. Am I saying, "I am limited to whatever may come."

David saw an issue that was not characteristic of whom he knew God to be and he sought after God for care and solutions.

Do we allow the Holy Spirit to direct our thoughts without arguing? When He directs us to conclude, as he directed David to conclude, that prolonged lack, want and excessive need is NOT characteristic of God, will we agree with Him? These questions must be answered to determine what actions we are willing to take in a time of lack.

Alright, back to David. What were the results of David's seeking the Lord?

First, David receives an immediate answer! He sought the Lord in order to discover the reason for the famine, and God responded.

V. 1b The LORD said, "It is on account of Saul and his blood-stained house; it is because he put the Gibeonites to death."

I want more "immediate" answers, how about you? The value of waiting is sometimes misapplied as an excuse for our not taking responsibility. If God doesn't want me to wait – then the issue is not Him, it's me. I am not saying that waiting never has a purpose. However, we see in scripture and in the example of Jesus' life – immediate answers can be a normal experience of the Christian life. Therefore we should never allow our previous experiences of not receiving immediate answers to override the facts of God's word.

Not only does David receive an immediate answer, he also receives the specific information that reveals the source/root of the extended famine.

*V. 1b The LORD said, "**It is on account of** Saul and his blood-stained house; **it is because** he put the Gibeonites to death."*

Who are these Gibeonites God speaks of and what do they have to do with the three years of famine? I encourage you to grab your bible and read Joshua Chapter 9:1-26 which tells us about the Gibeonites. These scriptures do not record all the details of Saul's motivation for his wrong act of ZEAL, but note Saul's failure to completely destroy the Amalekites. I believe his actions were an attempt to take matters into his own hands and try to maintain his position as king by an act of war; a war that God had **not** commanded him to initiate. When we live our lives from mere religious culture rather than from a personal relationship of trust and daily walking with God – we are left to attempt self-justification and self-protection. It is simple obedience to the One who loves us that will provide the divine revelation we desperately need.

*v. 2 The king (David) summoned the Gibeonites and spoke to them. (Now the Gibeonites were not a part of Israel but were survivors of the Amorites; **the Israelites had sworn to spare them**, **but Saul in his** **ZEAL** for Israel and Judah had tried to annihilate them.) v. 3 David asked* *the Gibeonites, "What shall I do for you? How shall I make amends so that you will bless the LORD's inheritance?"*

It had been divinely recorded in heaven and earth that the Gibeonites were to be allowed to live among the Israelites. A man (Saul) had ignored what God had asked of him. A nation (Israel) had bound themselves by oath to how they would treat another people group. "Past" actions were the reason for this time of famine in Israel. David was shown that ***thirteen generations earlier***, commitments were made that were having direct spiritual and physical implications in the "present". This is an incredible example of *generational sin, ungodly vows and living under a self-inflicted curse.*

> *Because David sought the Lord:*
> He is given insight and understands what he and the nation of Israel are accountable to address!

David asked those sinned against, "What will make atonement for all the injustice, all the pain, and all the loss created by Israel's past actions? Here we see David using his delegated reign to bring justice for a people that God had intended His nation to protect.

v. 4 The Gibeonites answered him, "We have no right to demand silver or gold from Saul or his family, nor do we have the right to put anyone in Israel to death." "What do you want me to do for you?" David asked. v. 5 They answered the king, "As for the man who destroyed us and plotted against us so that we have been decimated and have no place anywhere in Israel, v. 6 let seven of his male descendants be given to us to be killed and exposed before the LORD at Gibeah of Saul—the Lord 's chosen one." So the king said, "I will give them to you."

The answer to David's question regarding what could make atonement is clear: the shedding of blood.

King David agrees and recognizes that this is the true source of atonement. The shedding of blood is settlement for injustice and sin. The king did not refuse the request of the Gibeonites. They informed David they were exercising their right as "blood-avengers" for the cruelty committed on their ancestors. Up until the king's request they had not demanded satisfaction.

They specified seven descendants of Saul. This numerically represented "full and complete" consummation. Remember Jesus' words on the cross when he proclaimed "It is finished." ***<u>It is finished</u>*** is translated from the single Greek word *tetelestai*. It is an accounting term that means "paid in full." Full and complete reconciliation and resolution demands payment. And so, David says to the Gibeonites "I will give them to you."

Jesus is the true source of our atonement and reconciliation. The King of kings says "I will give myself for you and all mankind." His shed blood has been, is, and always will be the means of our forgiveness. His shed blood is our only source of redemption. He gives us new life.

v. 7 The king spared Mephibosheth son of Jonathan, the son of Saul, because of the oath before the LORD between David and Jonathan son of Saul. v. 8 But the king took..., the two sons of Rizpah... together with the five sons of Saul's daughter Merab, ... v. 9 He handed them over to the Gibeonites, who killed and exposed them on a hill before the LORD. All seven of them fell together; they were put to death during the first days of the harvest, just as the barley harvest was beginning..... v. 14 They buried the bones of Saul and his son Jonathan in the tomb of Saul's father Kish, at Zela in Benjamin, and did everything the king commanded. ***After that, God answered prayer in behalf of the land.***

IN SUMMARY WE MUST:

1) Recognize our responsibility to reign over your own lives through Him!
2) See our current circumstances in light of God's true character.
3) Express our desire to see God remove every obstacle.
4) Seek wisdom when we do not understand "why."
5) Determine to not self-justify and self-protect. Instead confess our sin and receive His forgiveness.
6) Expect change

CHAPTER 8

Our Co-Labor: Changing Time

If we would just have REAL REVIVAL!

PEOPLE WHO KNOW GOD AND HAVE ASKED TO BE SHOWN HIS WAYS…

> Gain the ability to intercede in a manner that not only produces results, but also influences conditions. This type of intercession can accelerate the time in which prayers are answered and influence a change in plans previously committed to.

Abraham, Isaac, Jacob, Moses, Samuel, Elijah, Elisha, Daniel, Hezekiah, David, Solomon, Mary, the Church in Jerusalem and the Church in Antioch are all examples of people interceding in ways that influenced change.

The following exchange between Mary and Jesus has tested my perspective on co-laboring with God regarding timing.

… a wedding took place at Cana in Galilee. Jesus' mother was there, and Jesus and his disciples had also been invited to the wedding. When the wine was gone, Jesus' mother said to him, "They have no

more wine." "Dear Woman, why do you involve me?" Jesus replied. "My hour has not yet come." His mother said to the servants, "Do whatever he tells you." Nearby stood six stone water jars, the kind used by the Jews for ceremonial washing, each holding from twenty to thirty gallons. Jesus said to the servants, "Fill the jars with water"; so they filled them to the brim. Then he told them, "Now draw some out and take it to the master of the banquet." They did so, and the master of the banquet tasted the water that had been turned into wine. He did not realize where it had come from, though the servants who had drawn the water knew. What Jesus did here in Cana of Galilee was the first of the signs through which he revealed his glory; and his disciples believed in him.

— JOHN 2:1-9A, 11

OBSERVATION 1:

Mary really knew Jesus

For 30 years Mary had treasured in her heart the words spoken to her about Jesus.

THE WORDS SPOKEN TO MARY:

Angel Gabriel:
..., God sent the angel Gabriel..., to a virgin.... The virgin's name was Mary. The angel went to her and said, "Greetings, you who are highly favored! The Lord is with you....You will conceive and give birth to a son, and you are to call him Jesus. He will be great and will be called the Son of the Most High. The Lord God will give him the throne of his father David, and he will reign over Jacob's descendants

forever; his kingdom will never end..., The Holy Spirit will come on you, and the power of the Most High will overshadow you. So the holy one to be born will be called the Son of God.... For no word from God will ever fail."

— LUKE 1:26-28, 33, 35, 36-37

Simeon:

Now there was a man in Jerusalem called Simeon, who was righteous and devout. He was waiting for the consolation of Israel, and the Holy Spirit was on him. It had been revealed to him by the Holy Spirit that he would not die before he had seen the Lord's Messiah. Moved by the Spirit, he went into the temple courts. When the parents brought in the child Jesus to do for him what the custom of the Law required, Simeon took him in his ARMS AND PRAISED GOD, SAYING: "SOVEREIGN LORD, AS YOU HAVE PROMISED, *you may now dismiss your servant in peace. For my eyes have seen your salvation, which you have prepared in the sight of all nations: a light for revelation to the Gentiles, and the glory of your people Israel." The child's father and mother marveled at what was said about him. Then Simeon blessed them and said to Mary, his mother: "This child is destined to cause the falling and rising of many in Israel, and to be a sign that will be spoken against, so that the thoughts of many hearts will be revealed. And a sword will pierce your own soul too."*

— LUKE 2:25-35

Anna:

There was also a prophet, Anna, the daughter of Penuel, of the tribe of Asher.... She never left the temple but worshiped night and day, fasting and praying. Coming up to them (Mary, Joseph and Jesus) at that very moment, she gave thanks to God and spoke about the child to all who were looking forward to the redemption of Jerusalem.

— LUKE 2:36-38

Jesus:

When his parents saw him, they were astonished. His mother said to him, "Son, why have you treated us like this? Your father and I have been anxiously searching for you." "Why were you searching for me?" he asked. "Didn't you know I had to be in my Father's house?" .... But his mother treasured all these things in her heart.

— LUKE 2:48-49, 51

OBSERVATION 2:

Mary asked because she really knew Jesus

Mary had many years to observe the servant heart of Jesus. Mary **knew** Jesus. She **knew** His predisposition to care for and serve others, so she brought Him the needs of the wedding hosts. *"They have no more wine."*

THE HEART OF A SERVANT:

For even the Son of Man did not come to be served, but to serve, and to give his life as a ransom for many.

— MARK 10:45

For who is greater, the one who is at the table or the one who serves? Is it not the one who is at the table? But I am among you as one who serves.

— LUKE 22:27

> *When he had finished washing their feet, he put on his clothes and returned to his place. "Do you understand what I have done for you?" he asked them. "You call me 'Teacher' and 'Lord,' and rightly so, for that is what I am. Now that I, your Lord and Teacher, have washed your feet, you also should wash one another's feet. I have set you an example that you should do as I have done for you.*
>
> — JOHN 13:12-15

OBSERVATION 3:

Mary recognized Jesus's NO may not mean NO because she really knew Jesus.

Jesus makes a clear statement regarding timing:

"My hour has not yet come."

WHAT HOUR:

What HOUR was Jesus referring to? Thayer's Greek Lexicon defines the word **hour** as: *a definite time, a point in time, an exact moment.* It has the meaning of being the opportune or appointed time.

This same word for ***hour*** is used in Revelation 14:7

> *He said in a loud voice, "Fear God and give him glory, because the* ***hour*** *of his judgment has come. Worship him who made the heavens, the earth, the sea and the springs of water."*

Also in Revelation 3:10

*"Since you have kept my command to endure patiently, I will also keep you from the **hour** of trial that is going to come on the whole world to test the inhabitants of the earth."*

And again in John 13:1

*It was just before the Passover Festival. Jesus knew that the **hour** had come for him to leave this world and go to the Father. Having loved his own who were in the world, he loved them to the end.*

Did Mary understand this reference to timing? Did she comprehend that Jesus was clearly stating it was ***not* the appointed time** for what she was requesting?

OBSERVATION 4:

Mary acknowledged Jesus's basis of operation because she really knew Jesus.

Jesus always operated under the following premise:

Jesus gave them this answer: "Very truly I tell you, the Son can do nothing by himself; he can do only what he sees his Father doing, because whatever the Father does the Son also does.

— JOHN 5:19

....I love the Father and do exactly what my Father has commanded me.

—JOHN 14:31B

In John 2:4 Jesus stated that His time had not yet come. In other words, based on the premise that He always functioned by the times the Father appointed, it was not time to start His miracle ministry.

So now we are faced with the following questions:

a) Was Jesus mistaken about the Father's timing when He said His hour had not yet come?

OR

b) Was Jesus disobeying the Father when He acted on Mary's request?

OR

c) Had the appointed time changed in that very moment?

A CHANGE IN TIME

If the appointed time did change, what caused the change?

My proposition is that Mary not only approached Jesus to insist that He take His proper role as her eldest son; but also because she knew who He was. She was recalling all the words of promise and prophesy spoken to her regarding Him. She remembered the Angel Gabriel's words and the overshadowing power of the Holy Spirit when chosen to carry the Son of God. All of these factors persuaded her to request, even after being told NO. Her faith spoke the following words, ***"Do whatever he tells you."***

Perhaps both the Father and the Son agreed that Mary could no longer bear the “weight of waiting” for Jesus to be revealed as the Messiah. Perhaps They saw this as the moment prophesied by Simeon in Luke 2:35?

“And a sword will pierce your own soul too.”

Perhaps They knew she was tempted to give up her faith? Perhaps her heavenly Father was fulfilling His Word recorded in 1 Corinthians 10:13b.

> *And God is faithful; he will not let you be tempted beyond what you can bear. But when you are tempted, he will also provide a way out so that you can endure it.*

Perhaps all these factors contributed to this change in God’s appointed timing. Did ***MARY*** influence the timing of this 1st miracle?

If YES, then she is an example of CO-LABORING with God. Timing was altered due to God’s Heart towards Mary and her longing for the ***time to be now!***

CHAPTER 9

Our Co-Labor: Changing Plans

If we would just have REAL REVIVAL!

<u>OH PROMISED LAND</u>

Oh promised land
Beholding my heart in your bosom
Engraving my name on your soil
Oh promise me…

Take my soul to the top of your mountains
Lead my heart to the depth of your seas
Hold my hand on this journey
As you promise me…

How we ache to return
Your people
Your spirit
How we enslave ourselves
To your promise…

Oh promised land!

Excerpts from <u>*Promised Land*</u> by Adele Hattingh.[1]

Just as Mary co-labored for ***timing***, Moses and David co-labored for a change in ***plans.***

A CHANGE IN PLANS:

MOSES AND A SEPARATION

Exodus chapter 3 and chapter 33 helps me to understand how we can co-labor with the Lord and His plans.

The Lord spoke the following to Moses in Exodus 3:16-17, 21-22a

> *"Now go and call together all the leaders of Israel. Tell them, 'The LORD, the God of your ancestors – the God of Abraham, Isaac, and Jacob – appeared to me in a burning bush. He said, "You can be sure that I am watching over you and have seen what is happening to you in Egypt. I promise to rescue you from the oppression of the Egyptians. I will lead you to the land now occupied by the Canaanites, Hittites, Amorites, Perizzites, Hivites, and Jebusites – a land flowing with milk and honey."' .... And I will see to it that the Egyptians treat you well. They will load you down with gifts so you will not leave empty-handed. The Israelite women will ask for silver and gold jewelry and articles of silver and gold and fine clothing from their Egyptian neighbors and their neighbors' guests...."*

Also in Exodus 33: 1-3 we read

> *Then the Lord said to Moses, "Leave this place,* (Mount Sinai) *you and the people you brought up out of Egypt, and go up to the land I promised on oath to Abraham, Isaac and Jacob, saying, 'I will give it to your descendants.' I will send an angel before you and drive out the Canaanites, Amorites,*

Hittites, Perizzites, Hivites and Jebusites. Go up to the land flowing with milk and honey.

THE GOOD NEWS FROM GOD'S PERSPECTIVE:

In these verses we see 10 remarkable statements spoken by God.

- I AM WATCHING OVER YOU.
- I HAVE SEEN WHAT IS HAPPENING TO YOU.
- I PROMISE TO RESCUE YOU.
- I WILL LEAD YOU.
- I WILL SEE THAT YOU DON'T LEAVE EMPTY HANDED.
- LEAVE WHERE YOU ARE NOW AND GO TO THE LAND I PROMISED.
- I WILL GIVE YOUR DESCENDANTS AN INHERITANCE.
- I WILL COMMAND ANGELIC HELP FOR YOU.
- ALL YOUR ENEMIES WILL BE REMOVED.
- GO NOW TO A WELL PREPARED AND FERTILE LAND.

Take a moment and envision the Lord stating these 10 things to you. Pause and picture your family being promised these words. What would the impact be on you? Would this encourage you? Would these direct statements from God be a source of joy and gratefulness? I would expect the Hebrew people to be extremely thankful and respond in celebration. Exodus chapter 33:4 records their response:

*When the people heard these **distressing words**, they began to mourn and no one put on any ornaments.*

The English Standard Version states it this way:

*When the people heard this **disastrous word**, they mourned, and no one put on his ornaments.*

What distressing words? What disastrous word? Please read the second part of Exodus chapter 33 verse 3,

But I will not go with you, because you are a stiff-necked people and I might destroy you on the way."

It appears that the people were beginning to perceive that regardless of all the GOOD things God would do for them – something of GREATER GOOD was being taken away. God Himself was no longer going to be with them in His abiding manifest presence. He was no longer going to PERSONALLY accompany them on their divine journey. These are the words that were distressing and disastrous to them! The primary reason for their response is they did not want to lose God being with them.

Getting back to our story in Exodus 33, you may be wondering why the people removed their articles of jewelry/ornaments in response to the discouraging news.

Exodus 32: 1-4 gives us insight.

When the people saw that Moses was so long in coming down from the mountain, they gathered around Aaron and said, "Come, make us gods who will go before us. As for this fellow Moses who

> *brought us up out of Egypt, we don't know what has happened to him." Aaron answered them, "**Take off the gold earrings that your wives, your sons and your daughters are wearing**, and bring them to me." **So all the people took off their earrings and brought them to Aaron. He took what they handed him and made it into an idol** cast in the shape of a calf, fashioning it with a tool. Then they said, "These are your gods, Israel, who brought you up out of Egypt."*

Do you recall

> "*... And I will see to it that the Egyptians treat you well. They will load you down with gifts so you will not leave empty-handed. The Israelite women will ask for silver and **gold jewelry and articles of silver and gold** and fine clothing from their Egyptian neighbors and their neighbors' guests...."*

In a moment of fear the Hebrews demanded a substitute for God's leadership. They wanted an idol that they could interact with on their own terms. They believed that this would give them the security they needed in that moment. If they could just touch their culturally created golden idol, perhaps it would alleviate their fears. They also threw a party to forget about life for a while.

The silver, gold and other resources that God had provided for them through the Egyptians, were intended to be a blessing. But they were now dedicating them to create a false, failing and fruitless god. When they came to their senses, they recognized that they had used their jewelry to create an object of adultery. They broke the heart of their true God and their adultery had provoked Him to anger.

I Will Not Go With You! Could these words spoken by God be changed? Could WHO Moses was influence God to change His stated plans?

> *Whenever the people saw the pillar of cloud standing at the entrance to the tent, they all stood and worshiped, each at the entrance to their tent. The Lord would speak to Moses face to face, as one speaks to a friend.*
>
> *Then Moses said to him, "If your Presence does not go with us, do not send us up from here. How will anyone know that you are pleased with me and with your people unless you go with us? What else will distinguish me and your people from all the other people on the face of the earth?"* ***And the Lord said to Moses, "I will do the very thing you have asked, because I am pleased with you and I know you by name."***
>
> — EXODUS 33: 10-11A, 15-17

It is important to remember that if we truly wish to co-labor with God the way He intends, we must ***know*** Him and ***please*** Him. God changed His plans because Moses possessed both of these qualities.

A CHANGE IN PLANS:

DAVID & A HOME

The book of 1 Chronicles contains another helpful story and illustrates how we can co-labor with the Lord and His plans.

> *After David was settled in his palace, he said to Nathan the prophet, "Here I am, living in a house*

of cedar, while the ark of the covenant of the Lord is under a tent." Nathan replied to David, "Whatever ***you have in mind****, do it, for God is with you." But that night the word of God came to Nathan, saying: "Go and tell my servant David, 'This is what the Lord says: You are not the one to build me a house to dwell in. I have not dwelt in a house from the day I brought Israel up out of Egypt to this day. I have moved from one tent site to another, from one dwelling place to another. Wherever I have moved with all the Israelites,* ***did I ever say*** *to any of their leaders whom I commanded to shepherd my people,* ***"Why have you not built me a house of cedar?"****'*

— 1 CHRONICLES 17: 1-6

David had a desire. According to what we just read, this desire was a thought in ***his*** mind and an emotion in ***his*** heart. He wanted the Lord to have a great temple for His dwelling. After all, he reasoned, even "*I am living in a house of cedar.*"

These Scriptures are crystal clear; God had never asked or instructed anyone to build Him a house on earth other than the tent of meeting and the Ark of the Covenant. His desire was to always lead and move with His people via the tabernacle.

But just as with Moses, because God was pleased with and knew David, He moves according to David's desire.

God fulfills the longing of David's heart on many levels.

- First, Because of WHO GOD IS - He can't help but turn the tables on David and bless his future.
- Then, if that was not enough, He blesses the people David leads.
- Still not done, He blesses David's family line.
- And finally, He blesses David's desire!

Now I will make your name like the names of the greatest men on earth. And I will provide a place for my people Israel and will plant them so that they can have a home of their own and no longer be disturbed. Wicked people will not oppress them anymore, as they did at the beginning and have done ever since the time I appointed leaders over my people Israel. I will also subdue all your enemies.

"'I declare to you that the Lord will build a house for you: When your days are over and you go to be with your ancestors, I will raise up your offspring to succeed you, one of your own sons, and I will establish his kingdom. He is the one who will build a house for me, and I will establish his throne forever. I will be his father, and he will be my son.'"

— 1 CHRONICLES 17: 8B-14

Later, in excerpts from 1 Chronicles 22: 5-10 we read:

David said, "My son Solomon is young and inexperienced, and the house to be built for the Lord should be of great magnificence and fame and splendor in the sight of all the nations. Therefore I *will make preparations for it." So David made extensive preparations before his death. David said to Solomon: "My son, **I had it in my heart** to build a house for the Name of the Lord my God. 8 But this word of the Lord came to me: ... 'You are not to build a house for my Name.... But you will have a son.... His name will be Solomon,.... He is the one who will build a house for my Name.*

DAVID WAS THE HEART OF THE MATTER

David himself was the heart of the matter. It was his desire and dream that created the temple of God.

> ***I had it in my heart*** *to build a house for the Name of the Lord my God.*

I once heard Bill Johnson, Pastor of Bethel Church in Redding, California comment on this passage. I paraphrase him:

> **Building the temple was in David's heart.**
> **Building David was in God's heart!**

This concept of co-laboring with God should redefine our definition of sovereignty. As I stated earlier, it is important that you and I not apply a definition of God's sovereignty that is counterproductive with His purposes!

Relegating all aspects of responsibility for awakenings, outpourings and revivals to God, apart from our participation, is not biblical; nor mature. We should no longer surrender the desires and dreams God has placed within us. We should not let these desires and dreams be lost to a theological comfort zone of our own creation. A world of our own making where nothing is ever expected to change.

Just as God created Mary, Moses and David, He has created you and me. He longs for our co-labor and friendship.

Jesus said ***I no longer call you Servants, now I call you Friends!*** Friends are informed about and understand the family business. Friends understand the character and heart of God. Friends are not only obedient – they bring joy and fulfillment to their Lord. Friends of God are more concerned with not disappointing Him than simply disobeying Him.

May God continue to teach us His ways! May we commit to apply what He teaches us! I know what I just said may seem harsh, but the alternative is a deathly form of Christian living.

Yes, only God knows the perfect time that a person, family, church, city, village, or nation is prepared for His outpourings. But we can and must:

- Maintain personal revival (*chapters 1 - 4*)
- Recognize God's revealed Conditions & Consequences (*chapter 5*)
- Recognize God's revealed Character & Concern (*chapter 6*)
- Recognize Our required Co-Labor (*chapters 7, 8 and 9*)

If we do these, God may very well give us the **<u>fruits</u>** of revival that we long for sooner!

CHAPTER 10

Information vs. Impartation

If we would just have REAL REVIVAL!

INFORMATION AND IMPARTATION!

A friend whom I had asked to review my notes for the writing of this book asked me the following question:

> *How do you actually pray for this stuff? What do you ask the Father for as you intercede for real moves of God?*

Or, in other words, ***Thanks for the Information, but I need some Impartation!***

First, I do **not** want us to miss the fact that my friend's question, in and of itself, reveals that she has progressed in her mindset. She is experiencing a paradigm shift. She has moved from:

"We really have no influence in determining spiritual outcomes"

to

"How do I apply these concepts and move the heart of God?"

She is applying the Biblical mandate to ponder, consider, examine, and even wrestle with what she had read. She is responsibly asking God if He wants her to make use of these concepts. If He says "Yes," then how does He want her to apply them?

She knew the Bible was clear about the power of a compassionate heart that prays. But now she is becoming familiar with the conflict that God so wisely and caringly balances. The Lord hears our prayers for His visitations while ensuring a timing that prevents premature judgement.

I once heard James Goll, founder of Encounters Network, ask a group to consider the definition of "tipping point."

Webster's Dictionary defines a tipping point as:

> "*The critical point in a situation, process, or system, beyond which a significant and often unstoppable effect or change takes place.*"

Wikipedia adds,

> *"A tipping point is a point in time when a group - or a large number of group members - rapidly and dramatically changes its behavior by widely adopting a previously rare practice. This phrase was first used in physics where it referred to the adding a small amount of weight to a balanced object until the additional weight caused the object to suddenly topple over or tip."*

At the end of James Goll's discussion, he shared the following two experiences. In a dream, he was standing on dry parched ground that was longing for moisture and relief. He saw raindrops falling from heaven and when each drop hit the earth, he heard a sound. With each drop that fell, he heard the word “Awake.” Another drop came, then another, with the same word “Awake” each time upon contact. As the rain continued to increase the sound shifted from “Awake” to “Awaken” and eventually to “Awakening.”

That same week he had a second experience. He said that the presence of the Lord came upon him for 8 hours until 4:00 a.m.. Eventually he fell asleep but was awakened by the voice of the Lord at 8:00 a.m. He heard a soothing voice say, “You know what I do with your tears, don’t you? I store them up in my bottles in heaven. When they are full, I then turn them upside down and they become the next raindrops from heaven falling upon parched hearts and dry ground. Your tears become My next outpouring. *You have taken account of my wanderings; Put my tears in Your bottle. Are they not recorded in Your book?”* (Psalm 56:8 AMP).

Our Prayers - Tipping Point for Revival:

> *I wonder Lord, if we are at a tipping point? Are You ready to release all of heaven for us, our families, friends, neighbors, churches, cities, states, and nations? Are you waiting for our collective cries to tip over on earth Your revival, restoration and recovery to come forth. Lord, speak to all of us, what would you have us do?*

Matthew Henry, an English theologian declared, *“When God intends to do great mercy for his people, the first thing He does is to set them a-praying!”*

S. D. Gordon stated, *“The greatest thing anyone can do for God and man is pray. It is not the only thing; but it is the chief thing. The great people of the earth today are the people who pray. I do not mean those who talk about prayer; not those who can explain about prayer; but I mean those people who take time and pray."*

Charles Finney, who was known for his phenomenal evangelistic successes during the Second Great Awakening, had the prayer support of Father Nash. He stated, *"Revival is no more a miracle than a crop of wheat. Revival comes from heaven when heroic souls enter the conflict determined to win or die - or if need be, - to win AND die."*

We all pray for lots of things, but the emphasis of this book is to encourage targeted daily prayer for revival and awakening.

When people ask me how I apply the concepts in this book to my daily prayer life, I say, "Come with me and pray." Those that have taken me up on my invitation are usually surprised by how brief and how direct I am when talking to God regarding His desire to visit us.

Please do not use any of the prayer examples provided in a legalistic manner. Do not view them as a self-imposed formula. An inflexible routine of words that ignores the leading and unction of the Holy Spirit during prayer will not bring life. You will only find assurance and confidence in your prayer life AS YOU PRAY!!

> *This is the confidence we have in approaching God: that if we ask anything according to his will, he hears us. And if we know that he hears us—whatever we ask—we know that we have what we asked of him.*
>
> —I JOHN 5:14-15

<u>WHAT WE NEED TO REMEMBER BEFORE WE PRAY:</u>

Individual and corporate conditions of accountability are created when God's words and God's miracles are present.

With God's manifest presence there is increased anointing on words spoken (preached, taught and communicated).

With God's manifest presence there is increased power displayed (salvation, healings, deliverances, miracles, signs, and wonders).

These increases create individual and corporate responsibility and accountability.

Saying "No" or choosing to walk away from God has consequences that were not present prior to hearing and seeing!

If we do not respond appropriately at these times of outpouring, the heart of God the Father is grieved. God is obligated to act out of who HE IS – not only a Loving Father – but also a Righteous Judge!

<u>He desires</u> to releases a move of His Holy Spirit in response to the prayers of His people.

<u>He knows</u> the potential for harm for those who hear and see if they are not prepared to respond appropriately.

<u>SAMPLE PRAYERS FOR A MOVE OF GOD</u>

SAMPLE 1**:** <u>Prayer for Self</u>:

FATHER, THANK YOU THAT YOU KNOW THE TRUE CONDITION OF MY HEART AT THIS VERY MOMENT. YOU KNOW MY MOTIVES, MY THOUGHTS, MY EMOTIONS, AND MY PERCEPTIONS. LORD, PLEASE GIVE ME THE POWER TO PURSUE AND MAINTAIN PERSONAL REVIVAL IN OUR RELATIONSHIP. I COME ASKING YOU TO FILL ME DAILY. KEEP MY LIFE REVIVED AND PROTECT MY FIRST LOVE FOR YOU.

SAMPLE 2**:** <u>Prayer for Family</u>:

FATHER, YOU SAID I DO NOT NEED TO WAIT ANOTHER FOUR MONTHS FOR HARVEST. YOU TOLD ME TO LOOK UP AND SEE THAT THE FIELDS ARE READY NOW. I AGREE WITH YOU LORD AND I ASK YOU FOR A CHANGE IN HARVEST TIME. I ASK THAT NOW BE THE TIME, NOT LATER. LORD, ON THE AUTHORITY OF YOUR WORD, YOUR NAME, AND YOUR INVITATION:

- I ASK YOU TO PREPARE MY FAMILY'S HEARTS TO SEE AND EXPERIENCE YOUR WORDS AND DEEDS. I ASK THAT YOU POSITION THEIR HEARTS TO RESPOND AS YOU RELEASE YOUR SPIRIT TO MOVE.
- I ASK YOU TO ACCELERATE THE CONDITION OF MY FAMILY'S HEARTS AND READINESS.
- I ASK YOU TO GIVE THEM THE MERCY, GRACE, POWER, WISDOM, PROVISION, AND PROTECTION THAT THEY NEED.

- LORD I ASK THAT EACH ONE COME TO A PERSONAL SAVING RELATIONSHIP WITH YOU AND THAT YOU FILL EACH OF THEM WITH YOUR HOLY SPIRIT.

SAMPLE 3**:** Prayer for YOUR Church:

FATHER, BIRTH AND MAINTAIN IN YOUR CHURCH THE POWER TO PRAY.

- I ASK THAT YOU PREPARE AND POSITION OUR HEARTS TO SAFELY SEE AND EXPERIENCE YOUR WORDS AND DEEDS.
- I ASK THAT YOU SEARCH OUR HEARTS AND CLEANSE US. LORD, GIVE US YOUR POWER TO CONFESS, REPENT AND BE CHANGED.
- REVEAL WHERE WE ARE PREVENTING YOU FROM ENTRUSTING US WITH REVIVAL AND AWAKENING.
- GOD FREE US, CREATE IN US A CLEAN HEART THAT YOU DESIRE TO REPRODUCE IN OTHERS.

A DREAM

I had an interesting dream while writing this book. I was in an auditorium during a time of worship. The music being played and the lyrics being sung, while magnificent, were completely new to me. I had never heard these songs before. However, I found that as the songs were being played and sung - I knew the lyrics at the precise moment they were to be expressed. At first I had insecure feelings and wondered if I could trust my impressions of the words. Over and over, each time, I simply “knew” the verses when I needed to. I soon began to relax and be consumed in how beautiful and deep this worship of the Lord was.

I then moved to a more open area of the auditorium to pray. As I was on my knees a young man wearing very dark black sunglasses came behind me and draped all the weight of his body over my head and shoulders. It became extremely uncomfortable and even painful. He then stated, “You always blame others, this must stop, you must be delivered.” I responded, “Did you ask my permission? You are being rude and the unbelievers will know that you are rude!” His friends said to him, “You have to stop this and get off, you are hurting him.” Then a young boy dressed in a Boy Scouts uniform said to me, “Tell him you need a house.” The boy and I laughed together as I told the man draped over me that I needed a house – the man suddenly was gone.

That evening when I woke up, I pondered this dream with the Lord. I was impressed that it related to the writing of this book.

This is what the dream means to me:

Real, God-given revival creates in us an ability to worship and express ourselves from a place of His strength and anointing.

At first, we are insecure and wonder if we can trust in the capabilities He is providing in the moment. We are tempted to trust in our own self effort again. We briefly fear not being in control.

Then, as we begin to enter a flow and experience the words of life He is giving, we choose to be at peace, relax and enter into His provision. Even though all of this is new to us, we have received an anointing to participate.

Next, we are stirred to pull aside and draw even nearer to God and pray. We are about to intercede. However, God wants us to intercede effectively – so He reveals a blind spot of sin in us. We feel the pain of this sin. It is a burden being carried that is not of God. Its dark glasses (blindness) and voice (accusation) weighs us down until God brings this revelation:

> *As you pray for revival you hold hidden resentments and accusations towards others in your heart. You have believed that "they" are the reason revival isn't coming.*

We place blame upon our parents, our husbands, our wives, our children, our church, other churches, our pastors, other pastors, this ministry, that ministry, this brother, that sister, the current president, the president's family, the federal government, congress, the supreme court, school boards, the NAACP, the ACLU, the ILGA, the police, Afro Americans, Whites, Hispanics, Asians, Gays, Lesbians, Trans-genders, Arabs, Israelis, the G8, the rich, those on welfare, etc., etc., etc.

In the dream, a demonic accusatory / blaming spirit of hell drapes over us and presses down harder and harder. We ask this oppressive spirit, "Did you ask my permission?" The answer is obvious. Whether we realize it or not, we gave it permission to operate in us by joining with its accusatory voice and character! We opened the door and invited a religious, self – righteous spirit to speak judgement through our "prayers". We joined the voice of the accuser as we prayed (Revelation 12:10).

> *You, therefore, have no excuse, you who pass judgment on someone else, for at whatever point you judge another, you are condemning yourself, because you who pass judgment do the same things. Now we know that God's judgment against those who do such things is based on truth. So when you, a mere human being, pass judgment on them and yet do the same things, do you think you will escape God's judgment? Or do you show contempt for the riches of his kindness, forbearance and patience, not realizing that God's kindness is intended to lead you to repentance?*
>
> — ROMANS 2:1-4

Providentially, wise and caring members of the body of Christ confront this unholy spirit. They have discerned the crippling effect this spirit is having on our ability to pray for real revival. They state, *"You have to stop this and get off, you are hurting him."* These faithful friends expose our responsibility to repent of our ungodly judgements and accusations.

At the end of this dream, a courageous and fun-loving child (to whom the Kingdom of God belongs) brings encouragement. He directs us to proclaim:

"We need a house."

But, why does he ask us to declare these words? Because…

> *Unless the Lord builds the house, those who build it labor in vain.*
>
> — PSALM 127:1A, ESV

This child of the Kingdom, dressed in uniform for faithful duty, has given us our freedom back. We needed this deliverance. The spirit of blindness and accusation that was operating in us has been removed!

This is my prayer for you, dear reader:

I pray that everything God has for you—all the personal revival you seek and need would be imparted to you each and every day. I pray the Lord makes certain you do not close the pages of this book without receiving all that is in His heart for you. I entrust you as a child into the arms of your Heavenly Father. I do this with full assurance that He will visit you and eternal fruits will be produced! May God give you His home, and may you faithfully invite others to come in and receive.

NOTES

Chapter 2
What Revival Is

1. Spurgeon, Charles Haddon. provided in the December 1866 Sword and Trowel http://www.spurgeon.org/s_and_t/wir1866.htm

2.GotQuestions.org, http://www.gotquestions.org/Christian-revival.html

Chapter 3
Tantalizing or Transforming

1. Kingdom of ***Heaven*** **vs.** Kingdom of ***God*** – why the difference? Are we talking about two different things?

The Hebrew word שמיים (shamayim), is what is known in Judaism as a כנוי (kinnui), or a "substitute," "nickname."

The reason why Matthew uses "kingdom of Heaven" here rather than "kingdom of God" is because he wrote to a Jewish audience, The Jews did not pronounce the ***Tetragrammaton יהוה*** :

Tet·ra·gram·ma·ton (tetrəˈgraməˌtän / noun): the Hebrew name of God transliterated in four letters as YHWH or JHVH and articulated as Yahweh or Jehovah. So as Rather than pronouncing the name of God, they used "substitutes, i.e. here "Heaven"

However, it can be seen that Kingdom of Heaven and the Kingdom of God refer to the same thing. "Kingdom of Heaven" is found 31 times, only in the Gospel of Matthew. "Kingdom of God" is found 62 times in ten books of the New Testament (Matthew, Mark, Luke, John, Acts, Romans, 1 Corinthians, Galatians, Colossians, and 2 Thessalonians). When the parallel accounts in the synoptic gospels are compared, whenever Matthew uses Kingdom of Heaven, the other will use Kingdom of God. Given the Jewish nature of Matthew's Gospel "Kingdom of Heaven" would be preferable for the author and his intended audience.

Chapter 5
His Character & His Concern

1. Bill Johnson, *Dreaming With God* (Shippensburg, PA: Destiny Image Publishers, 2006), p .60.

Chapter 8

Our Co-Labor: Changing Plans

1. Excerpts from *Promised Land* by Adele Hattingh, (http://www.chabad.org/theJewishWoman/article_cdo/aid/547251/jewish/Promised-Land.htm)

When Heaven Seems Silent:
How to Wait on God's Promises through Pain,
Disappointment, and Doubt

From Unspoken to Unbroken:
A Story of Hope - A Study in Healing

See other titles and free ***eBooks*** resources at:
www.handofjesus.org

www.ingramcontent.com/pod-product-compliance
Lightning Source LLC
LaVergne TN
LVHW010933110826
845149LV00013B/2574

* 9 7 8 0 9 8 9 3 8 1 5 5 0 *